# THE ULTIMATE
# PITTSBURGH PIRATES
# TRIVIA BOOK

## A Collection of Amazing Trivia Quizzes and Fun Facts for Die-Hard Pirates Fans!

**Ray Walker**

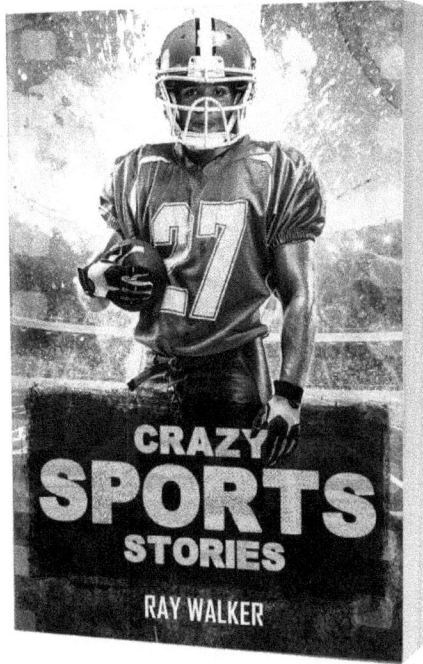

# CONTENTS

# INTRODUCTION

The Pittsburgh Pirates predate the MLB starting life being as Allegheny, of the American Association in 1881, before adding the Pittsburgh in front of their name in 1887, and finally in 1891 they started going by the name we know them by today. No matter their name, they have consistently proven themselves to be a team who fights hard and is a force to be reckoned with in the MLB.

Not a stranger to winning, some of the titles they hold, as of when this book was written in 2021, are 5 World Series Championships in 1909, 1925, 1960, 1971, and 1979 (which turned out to be their most recent visit), 9 National League pennants, 9 NL East Division titles, and 3 Wild Card berths. While the NL Central Division Championship title still remains elusive to them, they are often a threat in the division playing against teams like the St. Louis Cardinals, Cincinnati Reds, Chicago Cubs and Milwaukee Brewers.

Currently calling PNC Park, which opened in 2001, their home stadium, the Pittsburgh Pirates have retired the uniform numbers of Billy Meyer, Ralph Kiner, Willie Stargell, Bill Mazeroski, Paul Waner, Pie Traynor, Roberto Clemente,

Honus Wagner, Danny Murtaugh, and of course, Jackie Robinson.

The thing about baseball is that it is a lot like life. There are good times and bad times, good days, and bad days, but you have to do your absolute best to never give up. The Pittsburgh Pirates have proven that they refuse to give up and that they will do anything they need to do in order to bring a championship to the state of Pennsylvania. Winning is more than possible when you have a storied past like the Pittsburgh Pirates. They have so much captivating history and so many undeniable player legacies to be profoundly proud of.

With such a storied team past that goes back generations, you're probably already very knowledgeable as the die-hard Bucs fan that you are. Let's test that knowledge to see if you truly are the World's Biggest Pirates fan.

# CHAPTER 1:

# ORIGINS & HISTORY

## QUIZ TIME!

1. Which of the following team names did the Pirates franchise once go by?

   a. Pittsburgh Robbers

   b. Pittsburgh Alleghenys

   c. Pittsburgh Parrots

   d. They have always been the Pirates

2. In what year was the Pittsburgh Pirates franchise established?

   a. 1862

   b. 1872

   c. 1882

   d. 1892

3. The Pittsburgh Pirates' current home stadium is PNC Park.

   a. True

   b. False

4. Which division do the Pittsburgh Pirates play in currently?

    a. American League East
    b. American League Central
    c. National League Central
    d. National League East

5. The Pittsburgh Pirates have never won a Wild Card berth.

    a. True
    b. False

6. How many National League Pennants has the Pittsburgh Pirates franchise?

    a. 6
    b. 7
    c. 8
    d. 9

7. Who is the current principal owner of the Pittsburgh Pirates?

    a. Larry Dolan
    b. Robert Nutting
    c. Jim Pohlad
    d. Arturo Moreno

8. Who is the winningest manager in Pittsburgh Pirates history?

    a. Jim Leyland
    b. Danny Murtaugh
    c. Clint Hurdle
    d. Fred Clarke

9. What is the name of the Pittsburgh Pirates' Triple A-Team and where are they located?

   a. Indianapolis Indians
   b. Jacksonville Jumbo Shrimp
   c. Toledo Mud Hens
   d. St. Paul Saints

10. Who was the first manager of the Pittsburgh Pirates' franchise?

    a. Joe Battin
    b. Horace Phillips
    c. Al Pratt
    d. George Creamer

11. The Pittsburgh Pirates were members of the National League East division from 1969-1993.

    a. True
    b. False

12. What is the name of the Pittsburgh Pirates' current Spring Training home stadium?

    a. Roger Dean Chevrolet Stadium
    b. Hammond Stadium at CenturyLink Sports Complex
    c. Publix Field at Joker Marchant Stadium
    d. LECOM Park

13. How many appearances has the Pittsburgh Pirates franchise made in the MLB?

    a. 12
    b. 14

c. 17

d. 18

14. How many World Series titles have the Pittsburgh Pirates?

    a. 0

    b. 1

    c. 3

    d. 5

15. The Pittsburgh Pirates' current manager is Derek Shelton.

    a. True

    b. False

16. Which stadium was the first home stadium of the Pittsburgh Pirates franchise?

    a. Three Rivers Stadium

    b. Exposition Park III

    c. Exposition Park I, II

    d. Recreation Park

17. Who is the current General Manager of the Pittsburgh Pirates?

    a. Mike Rizzo

    b. Ben Cherington

    c. David Forst

    d. Thad Levine

18. How many National League Central Division titles have the Pittsburgh Pirates won?

    a. 0

    b. 2

c. 5

d. 7

19. The Pittsburgh Pirates won 9 National League East Division titles during their time in the NL East.

   a. True

   b. False

20. Travis Williams is the current President of the Pittsburgh Pirates

   a. True

   b. False

# QUIZ ANSWERS

1. B – Pittsburgh Alleghenys

2. C – 1882

3. A- True

4. C – National League Central

5. B – False, 3 (2013, 2014, 2015)

6. D – 9

7. B – Robert Nutting

8. D – Fred Clarke

9. A – Indianapolis Indians

10. C – Al Pratt

11. A – True

12. D – LECOM Park

13. C – 17

14. D – 5

15. A – True

16. C – Exposition Park I, II

17. B – Ben Cherington

18. A – 0

19. A – True

20. A – True

# DID YOU KNOW?

1. The Pittsburgh Pirates franchise has had 46 managers so far in their history. They include Al Pratt, Ormond Butler, Joe Battin, Denny McKnight, Bob Ferguson, George Creamer, Horace Phillips, Fred Dunlap, Ned Hanlon, Guy Hecker, Bill McGunnigle, Tom Burns, Al Buckenberger, Connie Mack, Patsy Donovan, Bill Watkins, Fred Clarke, Nixey Callahan, Honus Wagner, Hugo Bezdek, George Gibson, Bill McKechnie, Donie Bush, Jewel Ens, Pie Traynor, Frankie Frisch, Spud Davis, Billy Herman, Bill Burwell, Billy Meyer, Fred Haney, Bobby Bragan, Danny Murtaugh, Harry Walker, Larry Shepard, Alex Grammas, Bill Virdon, Chuck Tanner, Jim Leyland, Gene Lamont, Lloyd McClendon, Pete Mackanin, Jim Tracy, John Russell, Clint Hurdle, and Derek Shelton.

2. The Pittsburgh Pirates' current manager is Derek Shelton, he was a catcher in the MiLB in the early 1990s. In addition to coaching the Pirates from 2005-2019 he also coached for the Cleveland Indians, Tampa Bay Rays, Toronto Blue Jays, and Minnesota Twins. When he wasn't busy with baseball, he managed to get a degree from Southern Illinois University in Criminal Justice.

3. Fred Clarke is the Pittsburgh Pirates' all-time winningest manager with a record of 1,422-969 (.595) W-L%. Clarke managed the Pittsburgh Pirates from 1900-1915.

4. Robert Nutting is the current principal owner of the Pittsburgh Pirates. He is chairman of several ski resorts and CEO of Ogden Newspapers Inc.

5. The Pittsburgh Pirates franchise has hosted 5 MLB All-Star Games so far in their history; 1944, 1959 (Forbes Field), 1974, 1994 (Three Rivers Stadium), and 2006 (PNC Park).

6. The Pittsburgh Pirates have had 6 no-hitters thrown in franchise history. The first occurred in 1907, thrown by Nick Maddox and the latest occurred in 1997, thrown by Francisco Cordova and Ricardo Rincon. There have been no Perfect Games in Pittsburgh Pirates history so far.

7. The Pittsburgh Pirates won three consecutive Wild Card berths from 2013-2015.

8. The Pittsburgh Pirates' Double-A team is the Altoona Curve. High Single A is the Greensboro Grasshoppers. Low Single A is the Bradenton Marauders.

9. The Pittsburgh Pirates' current mascot is named "The Pirate Parrot".

10. The Pittsburgh Pirates have retired 9 numbers so far in franchise history, 10 including Jackie Robinson's No. 42, which is retired league wide. The latest Pirates player to have his number retired was Paul Waner in 2007.

# CHAPTER 2:

# JERSEYS & NUMBERS

## QUIZ TIME!

1. The Pittsburgh Pirates' original team colors were patriotic red, white, and blue.

   a. True
   b. False

2. What are the Pittsburgh Pirates' official team colors?

   a. White, Gold, Gray
   b. Black, Gold, Red
   c. Black, Gold, White
   d. Gold, Navy Blue, White

3. The Pittsburgh Pirates wore camo jerseys every Thursday home game during the 2015 MLB season to honor the Armed Forces.

   a. True
   b. False

4. Which of the following numbers in NOT retired by the Pittsburgh?

   a. 1
   b. 8
   c. 39
   d. 40

5. What uniform number does Colin Moran currently wear as a member of the Pittsburgh Pirates?

   a. 8
   b. 17
   c. 19
   d. 38

6. What uniform number did Jason Kendall wear during his time with the Pittsburgh Pirates?

   a. 8
   b. 18
   c. 28
   d. 38

7. Bob Friend wore the uniform numbers 25 and 19 during his time with the Pittsburgh Pirates.

   a. True
   b. False

8. Junior Ortiz, and which other player, are the only two Pittsburgh Pirates players to have ever worn the uniform No. 0 in franchise history?

a. Bill Baker

b. Joe Page

c. Rick White

d. U L Washington

9. Who is the only Pittsburgh Pirates player to have ever worn the uniform No. 80?

a. Rick White

b. Andrew Susac

c. Lastings Milledge

d. Jared Oliva

10. No Pittsburgh Pirates player has ever won the uniform No. 99.

a. True

b. False

11. What uniform number did Andrew McCutchen wear as a member of the Pittsburgh Pirates?

a. 2

b. 12

c. 22

d. 26

12. What uniform number did Bill Mazeroski wear as a member of the Pittsburgh Pirates?

a. 9

b. 19

c. 29

d. 39

13. Andy Van Slyke wore the uniform numbers 7 and 18 during his time with the Pittsburgh Pirates.

   a. True
   b. False

14. What uniform number did Vern Law wear as a member of the Pittsburgh Pirates?

   a. 10
   b. 20
   c. 32
   d. Both B & C

15. What uniform number did John Candelaria wear as a member of the Pittsburgh Pirates?

   a. 45
   b. 49
   c. 50
   d. All of the Above

16. What uniform number did Ralph Kiner wear as a member of the Pittsburgh Pirates?

   a. 4
   b. 14
   c. 43
   d. Both A & C

17. During his time with the Pittsburgh Pirates, Starling Marte wore which uniform number?

   a. 6
   b. 16

c. 26

d. 36

18. What uniform number did Jason Bay wear with the Pittsburgh Pirates?

    a. 28

    b. 38

    c. 48

    d. 58

19. What uniform number did Ryan Vogelsong wear as a member of the Pittsburgh Pirates?

    a. 14

    b. 22

    c. 28

    d. All of the Above

20. Barry Bonds wore the uniform numbers 7 and 24 during his time with the Pittsburgh Pirates.

    a. True

    b. False

# QUIZ ANSWERS

1. A - True

2. C – Black, Gold, White

3. A – True

4. C – 39

5. C – 19

6. B – 18

7. A – True

8. D – U L Washington

9. B – Andrew Susac

10. A – True

11. C – 22

12. A – 9

13. A – True

14. D – Both B & C

15. D – All of the Above

16. D – Both A & C

17. A – 6

18. B – 38

19. D – All of the Above

20. A – True

# DID YOU KNOW?

1. The Pittsburgh Pirates have retired 10 uniform numbers overall so far in franchise history, including Billy Meyer (No. 1), Ralph Kiner (No. 4), Willie Stargell (No. 8), Bill Mazeroski (No. 9), Paul Waner (No. 11), Pie Traynor (No. 20), Roberto Clemente (No. 21), Honus Wagner (No. 33), Danny Murtaugh (No. 40), and Jackie Robinson (No. 42).

2. During his time with the Pittsburgh Pirates, Paul Waner wore the uniform numbers 9 and 11.

3. Arky Vaughan wore the uniform numbers 3, 5, and 21 during his time with the Pittsburgh Pirates.

4. During his time with the Pittsburgh Pirates, A.J. Burnett wore the uniform number 34.

5. During his time with the Pittsburgh Pirates, Francisco Liriano wore the uniform number 47.

6. During his time with the Pittsburgh Pirates, Jason Grilli wore the uniform number 39.

7. Jackie Robinson's No. 42 is retired by the Pittsburgh Pirates as well as the MLB as a whole. No Pirates or MLB player will ever wear No. 42 again. The Yankees' Mariano Rivera was the final player to wear it.

8. During his time with the Pittsburgh Pirates, Jay Bell wore the uniform No. 3.

9.  During his time with the Pittsburgh Pirates, Jose Bautista wore the uniform numbers 7, 19, and 50.

10. Gregory Polanco currently wears the uniform No. 25 with the Pittsburgh Pirates.

# CHAPTER 3:

# ARRIBA

## QUIZ TIME!

1. What was Roberto Clemente's full name?

    a. Enrique Roberto Clemente Walker

    b. Roberto Enrique Clemente Walker

    c. Roberto Elias Clemente Walker

    d. Ernie Roberto Clemente Walker

2. Roberto Clemente played his entire 18-season MLB career with the Pittsburgh Pirates.

    a. True

    b. False

3. Where was Roberto Clemente born?

    a. Samana, Dominican Republic

    b. Santo Domingo, Dominican Republic

    c. San Juan, Puerto Rico

    d. Carolina, Puerto Rico

4. When was Roberto Clemente born?

a. April 18, 1934

b. April 18, 1944

c. August 18, 1934

d. August 18, 1944

5. Roberto Clemente did NOT win a World Series Championship during his time in the MLB.

a. True

b. False

6. How many MLB All-Star Games was Roberto Clemente named to over the course of his 18-season MLB career?

a. 5

b. 8

c. 10

d. 15

7. What year was Roberto Clemente inducted into the National Baseball Hall of Fame?

a. 1970

b. 1973

c. 1975

d. 1979

8. In 1958, Roberto Clemente enlisted in the United States Marine Corps. He served during baseball offseasons until 1964.

a. True

b. False

9. What was Roberto Clemente's career batting average?

   a. .287
   b. .297
   c. .307
   d. .317

10. What year was Roberto Clemente named the National League MVP?

   a. 1965
   b. 1966
   c. 1967
   d. 1969

11. How many Gold Glove Awards did Roberto Clemente win over the course of his 18-season MLB career?

   a. 10
   b. 11
   c. 12
   d. 13

12. Roberto Clemente was named the 1971 World Series MVP.

   a. True
   b. False

13. How many National League Batting Titles did Roberto Clemente win over the course of his 18-season MLB career?

   a. 1
   b. 2

c. 3

d. 4

14. Roberto Clemente was 20 years old when he made his MLB debut with the Pittsburgh Pirates.

    a. True

    b. False

15. How many total home runs did Roberto Clemente hit over the course of his 18-season MLB career?

    a. 220

    b. 230

    c. 240

    d. 250

16. How many total stolen bases did Roberto Clemente record over the course of his 18-season MLB career?

    a. 73

    b. 83

    c. 93

    d. 103

17. Roberto Clemente's career WAR is 94.8.

    a. True

    b. False

18. Over the course of his 18-season MLB career, how many times was Roberto Clemente named the NL Player of the Month?

    a. 1

    b. 2

c. 3

d. 4

19. How many hits did Roberto Clemente record over the course of his 18-season MLB career?

    a. 2,000

    b. 2, 100

    c. 2,500

    d. 3,000

20. Roberto Clemente's nephew, Edgard played in the MLB for three seasons.

    a. True

    b. False

# QUIZ ANSWERS

1. B – Roberto Enrique Clemente Walker

2. A – True

3. D – Carolina, Puerto Rico

4. C – August 18, 1934

5. B – False (2)

6. D – 15

7. B – 1973 (by special election)

8. A – True

9. D – .317

10. B – 1966

11. C – 12

12. A – True

13. D – 4

14. A – True

15. C – 240

16. B – 83

17. A - True

18. C – 3 (May 1960, May 1967, July 1969)

19. D – 3,000

20. A – True

# DID YOU KNOW?

1. In 1972, while on a charity relief flight to help Nicaragua after an earthquake, Roberto Clemente's plane crashed, killing him and others, and they were never able to recover his remains. After Clemente's death, his wife Vera said he had always believed he would die young. It turns out he correct with his prediction, as he was only 38 years old at the time of his death.

2. Each year, the MLB gives out the 'Roberto Clemente Award' to a player who best exemplifies the playing spirit and community service that Clemente did while he was alive.

3. Roberto Clemente was the first Caribbean and Latino-American baseball player to be inducted into the National Baseball Hall of Fame.

4. Roberto Clemente's death led to a change in National Baseball Hall of Fame enshrinement rules. After his death, it was determined that in addition to a player being eligible 5 years after retirement, they could also be eligible 6 months after their death. A special election was held to enshrine Clemente after his untimely, tragic death.

5. Roberto Clemente was the youngest of seven children.

6. Roberto Clemente's uniform No. 23 was retired by the Pittsburgh Pirates on April 6, 1973.

7. Roberto Clemente claimed that being in the United States Marine Corps helped him gain 10 pounds of muscle and helped the back troubles he had acquired from a car accident disappear.

8. Roberto Clemente was inducted into the Marine Corps Sports Hall of Fame in 2003 and was inducted into the Puerto Rican Veterans Hall of Fame in 2018.

9. Roberto Clemente was a devout catholic throughout his life.

10. Roberto Clemente and his wife, Vera had three children, Roberto Jr., Luis Roberto, and Roberto Enrique. Vera Clemente died in November of 2019, at 78 years old.

# CHAPTER 4:

# CATCHY NICKNAMES

## QUIZ TIME!

1.  What nickname did Honus Wagner go by?

    a.  Nussie
    b.  The Flying Pennsylvanian
    c.  The Flying Dutchman
    d.  Waggie

2.  Roberto Clemente went by the nicknames "Arriba" and "The Great One".

    a.  True
    b.  False

3.  What nickname did Paul Waner go by?

    a.  Big Paul
    b.  Big Poison
    c.  Big Papa
    d.  Big Paulie

4.  What nickname did Willie Stargell go by?

a. Big Willie

b. Star

c. Pops

d. Gelly

5. "Arky" was a nickname. What was Arky Vaughan's full name?

a. Frederick Jacob Vaughan

b. Jacob Frederick Vaughan

c. Floyd Joseph Vaughan

d. Joseph Floyd Vaughan

6. Which nickname did Fred Clarke go by?

a. Crushin' Clarke

b. Hammer

c. Iron

d. Cap

7. Bob Friend went by the nickname "Warrior".

a. True

b. False

8. What nickname did Max Carey go by?

a. Big Max

b. Scoops

c. Maxi

d. Swing

9. What nickname does Bill Mazeroski go by?

a. Zero

b. Big Bill

c. Maz

d. Ski

10. "Pie" is a nickname. What is Pie Traynor's full name?

    a. Louis James Traynor

    b. James Louis Traynor

    c. Joseph Harold Traynor

    d. Harold Joseph Traynor

11. What nickname did Dave Parker go by?

    a. Anaconda

    b. Python

    c. Rattle

    d. Cobra

12. Sam Leever went by the nicknames "Deacon" and "The Goshen Schoolmaster".

    a. True

    b. False

13. Which nickname does John Candelaria go by?

    a. Candle Man

    b. Candy Man

    c. Dela

    d. Big J

14. What nickname does Vern Law go by?

    a. Deacon

    b. Preacher

    c. Lawyer

    d. Both A & B

15. Andy Van Slyke goes by the nickname "Slick".

    a. True
    b. False

16. What nickname does Andrew McCutchen go by?

    a. Cutch
    b. Big A
    c. Big Mac
    d. Uncle Drew

17. Jesse Tannehill went by the nicknames "Tanny" and "Powder".

    a. True
    b. False

18. What is Pedro Alvarez's nickname?

    a. El Tigre
    b. El Toro
    c. El León
    d. El Oso

19. What nickname does Russell Martin go by?

    a. Big Russ
    b. Muscle
    c. Brains
    d. Canada

20. Jason Grilli goes by the nickname "Grill Cheese".

    a. True
    b. False

# QUIZ ANSWERS

1. C – The Flying Dutchman

2. A- True

3. B – Big Poison

4. C – Pops

5. D – Joseph Floyd Vaughan

6. D – Cap

7. A – True

8. B – Scoops

9. C – Maz

10. D – Harold Joseph Traynor

11. D – Cobra

12. A – True

13. B – Candy Man

14. D – Both A & B

15. A - True

16. A – Cutch

17. A – True

18. B – El Toro

19. B – Muscle

20. A – True

# DID YOU KNOW?

1. Neil Walker goes by the nickname, "Walkie".

2. Josh Bell goes by the nickname, "JB".

3. Gregory Polcano goes by the nickname, "El Coffee".

4. Jordy Mercer goes by the nickname, "The Rook".

5. Francisco Cervelli goes by the nickname, "Cisco".

6. Ryan Vogelsong goes by the nickname, "Vogey".

7. Travis Snider goes by the nicknames, "Lunchbox".

8. Jose Bautista goes by the nickname, "Joey Bats".

9. "A.J." is a nickname. A.J. Burnett's full name is Allan James Burnett.

10. Bronson Arroyo goes by the nicknames, "Saturn Nuts", "Smokey", "Tacks", "Dirty", "BroYo" and "Free Love".

# CHAPTER 5:

# COBRA

## QUIZ TIME!

1. What is Dave Parker's full name?

   a. Gene David Parker

   b. David Gene Parker

   c. David Gregory Parker

   d. Gregory David Parker

2. Dave Parker played his entire 19-season MLB career with the Pittsburgh Pirates.

   a. True

   b. False

3. Where was Dave Parker born?

   a. Joplin, Missouri

   b. St. Louis, Missouri

   c. Tupelo, Mississippi

   d. Grenada, Mississippi

4. When was Dave Parker born?

a. January 9, 1951

b. January 9, 1961

c. June 9, 1951

d. June 9, 1961

5. Dave Parker was named the 1978 National League MVP.

   a. True

   b. False

6. How many total MLB All-Star Games was Dave Parker named to over the course of his 19-season MLB career?

   a. 5

   b. 7

   c. 9

   d. 11

7. How many Silver Slugger Awards did Dave Parker win over the course of his 19-season MLB career?

   a. 1

   b. 2

   c. 3

   d. 4

8. Dave Parker did NOT win a World Series Championship during his career.

   a. True

   b. False

9. What year was Dave Parker named the MLB All-Star Game MVP?

a.  1975

b.  1976

c.  1978

d.  1979

10. How many Gold Glove Awards did Dave Parker win over the course of his 19-season MLB career?

a.  0

b.  1

c.  c. 2

d.  d. 3

11. How many times did Dave Parker win the National League Batting Title over the course of his 19-season MLB career?

a.  0

b.  1

c.  2

d.  3

12. Dave Parker is a member of the National Baseball Hall of Fame.

a.  True

b.  False

13. What year did Dave Parker lead the National League in RBIs?

a.  1980

b.  1985

c.  1990

d.  1991

14. Dave Parker is a member of the Cincinnati Reds Hall of Fame.

    a. True
    b. False

15. How many total home runs did Dave Parker hit over the course of his 19-season MLB career?

    a. 339
    b. 349
    c. 359
    d. 369

16. Dave Parker won one World Series Championship with the Pittsburgh Pirates and one with which other team?

    a. Toronto Blue Jays
    b. Cincinnati Reds
    c. California Angels
    d. Oakland A's

17. Dave Parker's career batting average is .290.

    a. True
    b. False

18. How many total hits did Dave Parker collect over the course of his 19-season MLB career?

    a. 2,612
    b. 2,712
    c. 2,812
    d. 2,912

19. How many total stolen bases did Dave Parker collect over the course of his 19-season MLB career?

    a.  134

    b.  144

    c.  154

    d.  164

20. Dave Parker collected 1,493 RBIs over the course of his 19-season MLB career.

    a.  True

    b.  False

# QUIZ ANSWERS

1.  B – David Gene Parker

2.  B – False, Pirates, Cincinnati Reds, Oakland A's, California Angels, Toronto Blue Jays & Milwaukee Brewers

3.  D – Grenada, Mississippi

4.  C – June 9, 1951

5.  A – True

6.  B – 7

7.  C – 3

8.  B – False, 2

9.  D – 1979

10. D – 3

11. C – 2 (1977 & 1978)

12. A – True

13. B – 1985

14. A – True

15. A – 339

16. D – Oakland A's

17. A - True

18. B – 2,712

19. C – 154

20. A – True

# DID YOU KNOW?

1. Dave Parker's coaching career has included: Anaheim Angels First Base Coach, St. Louis Cardinals Batting Coach, and Pirates Special Hitting Instructor.

2. Dave Parker used to own several Popeye's Chicken chain restaurants throughout the Cincinnati area.

3. Dave Parker was diagnosed with Parkinson's Disease in 2013. His foundation, the Dave Parker 39 Foundation raises money in search for a cure.

4. Dave Parker was inducted into the Cincinnati Public Schools Athletic Hall of Fame in 2012.

5. While warming up in the on-deck circle, Dave Parker and his Pirates teammate, Willie Stargell would use a sledgehammer as opposed to a lead-weighted bat.

6. Dave Parker's cocaine use during his playing days was at the center of an MLB drug scandal during that time.

7. Dave Parker threw out 72 base runners between 1975-1979.

8. Dave Parker attended Courter Tech High School in Cincinnati, Ohio, and that is where his formal education ended, as he did not attend college.

9. Dave Parker wore the uniform No. 39 with every team he played with in his 19-season MLB career.

10. During a 1979 game, Dave Parker hit a ball so hard that half of the cover on the baseball came off and the seams on the ball were destroyed. This made it difficult to throw back to the infield.

# CHAPTER 6:

# STATISTICALLY SPEAKING

## QUIZ TIME!

1. Willie Stargell currently holds the Pittsburgh Pirates franchise record for the most home runs. How many home runs did he hit over the course of his MLB career?

    a. 455
    b. 465
    c. 475
    d. 485

2. Pitcher Wilbur Cooper has the most wins in Pittsburgh Pirates franchise history with 202 total.

    a. True
    b. False

3. Which pitcher holds the Pittsburgh Pirates record for most career shutouts thrown with 44?

    a. Vic Willis
    b. Bob Friend

c. Sam Leever

d. Babe Adams

4. Which Pittsburgh Pirates batter currently holds the single season record for strikeouts with 186?

a. Craig Wilson

b. Pedro Alvarez

c. Jason Bay

d. David Freese

5. Bob Friend has the most strikeouts in Pittsburgh Pirates franchise history with how many?

a. 1,482

b. 1,582

c. 1,682

d. 1,782

6. Who has the most stolen bases in Pittsburgh Pirates franchise history, with 688 total?

a. Honus Wagner

b. Barry Bonds

c. Omar Moreno

d. Max Carey

7. Roy Face holds the record for most saves in Pittsburgh Pirates history with 186 total.

a. True

b. False

8. Which player holds the Pittsburgh Pirates record for being intentionally walked, with 227 total?

a. Roberto Clemente

b. Willie Stargell

c. Barry Bonds

d. Dave Parker

9. Which player holds the Pittsburgh Pirates franchise record for home runs in a single season with 54 total?

a. Josh Bell

b. Brian Giles

c. Ralph Kiner

d. Willie Stargell

10. Which batter holds the single season Pittsburgh Pirates record for hits with 237 total?

a. Lloyd Waner

b. Paul Waner

c. Matty Alou

d. Jimmy Williams

11. Which player holds the single season Pittsburgh Pirates record for double plays grounded into with 25 total?

a. Tony Pena

b. Jose Castillo

c. Roberto Clemente

d. Al Todd

12. Willie Stargell holds the record for the most sacrifice flies in Pittsburgh Pirates all-time franchise history with 75 total.

a. True

b. False

13. Bob Veale threw the highest number of wild pitches in Pittsburgh Pirates franchise history with how many in total?

    a.  80
    b.  85
    c.  90
    d.  100

14. Holding the top spot in a single season for most triples in Pittsburgh Pirates history, how many did Chief Wilson hit in 1912?

    a.  30
    b.  36
    c.  38
    d.  40

15. Which hitter has the most walks in Pittsburgh Pirates franchise history with 937 total?

    a.  Max Carey
    b.  Paul Waner
    c.  Andrew McCutchen
    d.  Willie Stargell

16. Which Pittsburgh Pirates hitter holds the all-time franchise record for best overall batting average at .360?

    a.  Willie Stargell
    b.  Roberto Clemente
    c.  Jake Stenzel
    d.  Paul Waner

17. Honus Wagner holds the Pittsburgh Pirates record for most runs scored with 1,521 total.

    a. True
    b. False

18. How many plate appearances does Honus Wagner have to earn him the title of most plate appearances all time in Pittsburgh Pirates franchise history?

    a. 7, 228
    b. 8, 228
    c. 9, 228
    d. 10, 228

19. Which pitcher holds the Pittsburgh Pirates franchise record for most saves in a single season with 51 total?

    a. Mike Williams
    b. Mark Melancon
    c. Jason Grilli
    d. Jose Mesa

20. Bob Friend holds the Pittsburgh Pirates franchise record for most losses with 218 total.

    a. True
    b. False

# QUIZ ANSWERS

1. C – 475

2. A - True

3. D – Babe Adams

4. C – Pedro Alvarez (2013)

5. C – 1,682

6. D – Max Carey

7. A – True

8. B – Willie Stargell

9. D – Ralph Kiner (1949)

10. B – Paul Waner (1927)

11. D – Al Todd (1938)

12. A – True

13. C – 90

14. B – 36

15. D – Willie Stargell

16. C – Jake Stenzel

17. A – True

18. D – 10, 228

19. B – Mark Melancon (2015)

20. A – True

# DID YOU KNOW?

1. Bob Friend threw the most innings in Pittsburgh Pirates franchise history with 3,480.1 total. Coming in second is Wilbur Cooper who threw 3,199.0 innings total.

2. Arky Vaughan had the best single season batting average in Pittsburgh Pirates franchise history at .385 in 1935. Coming in second is Honus Wagner whose batting average was .381 in 1900.

3. Tony Womack holds the Pittsburgh Pirates franchise record for stolen base percentage with 89.05% accuracy. Max Carey holds the Pittsburgh Pirates franchise record for stolen bases with 688 total. Omar Moreno holds the Pittsburgh Pirates franchise record for the most times caught stealing at 137 times total.

4. Willie Stargell has the most extra-base hits in Pittsburgh Pirates franchise history with 953 total. Second on the list is Honus Wagner with 865 total.

5. Ralph Kiner holds the Pittsburgh Pirates franchise record for at-Bats per Home Run at 13.0. Essentially what this means is that on average, Kiner hit a home run about every 13 at-bats.

6. Francisco Liriano holds the Pittsburgh Pirates franchise record for strikeouts per 9 innings pitched at 9.368. Essentially what this means is that during his time with

the Bucs, Liriano recorded about 9-10 strikeouts in every 9 innings that he pitched.

7. Jason Kendall holds the single season Pittsburgh Pirates record for the most hit by pitches with 31 both in 1997 and 1998. Pink Hawley holds the single season Pittsburgh Pirates record for most batters hit with 33 in 1895.

8. Paul Waner holds the Pittsburgh Pirates franchise record for career doubles hit with 558 total. Second on the list is Honus Wagner with 551 total.

9. Ed Morris holds the Pittsburgh Pirates single season record for wins with 41 in 1886. Fleury Sullivan holds the Pittsburgh Pirates single season record for most losses with 35 in 1884.

10. Ed Morris holds the Pittsburgh Pirates franchise record for most strikeouts in a single season with 326 total in 1886.

# CHAPTER 7:

# THE TRADE MARKET

## QUIZ TIME!

1. On April 1, 1987, the Pittsburgh Pirates traded Tony Pena to which team, in exchange for Andy Van Slyke, Mike LaValliere and Mike Dunne?

   a. Baltimore Orioles
   b. St. Louis Cardinals
   c. Philadelphia Phillies
   d. Boston Red Sox

2. On January 30, 1959, the Pittsburgh Pirates traded Whammy Douglas, Jim Pendleton, John Powers and Frank Thomas to which team, in exchange for Harvey Haddix, Smoky Burgess and Don Hoak?

   a. Philadelphia Phillies
   b. Chicago White Sox
   c. Cincinnati Reds
   d. Chicago Cubs

3. The Pittsburgh Pirates have made 13 total trades with the Arizona Diamondbacks as of the end of the 2020 season.

   a. True
   b. False

4. On July 23, 1986, the Pittsburgh Pirates traded Jose DeLeon to the Chicago White Sox in exchange for which player?

   a. R.J. Reynolds
   b. Lee Mazzilli
   c. U L Washington
   d. Bobby Bonilla

5. The Pittsburgh Pirates have made only 5 trades with the Colorado Rockies all time (as of the end of 2020).

   a. True
   b. False

6. On November 26, 1986, the Pittsburgh Pirates traded Pat Clements, Cecilio Guante and Rick Rhoden to which team, in exchange for Doug Drabek, Logan Easley, and Brian Fisher?

   a. Chicago White Sox
   b. Houston Astros
   c. New York Yankees
   d. Baltimore Orioles

7. On November 18, 1998, the Pittsburgh Pirates traded Ricardo Rincon to the which team, in exchange for Brian Giles?

a. Oakland A's

b. Cleveland Indians

c. St. Louis Cardinals

d. Kansas City Royals

8. On August 26, 2003, the Pittsburgh Pirates traded Brian Giles to which team, in exchange for Jason Bay, Oliver Perez, and Cory Stewart?

a. Seattle Mariners

b. New York Mets

c. San Diego Padres

d. Boston Red Sox

9. On July 23, 2003, the Pittsburgh Pirates traded Aramis Ramirez, Kenny Lofton, and cash considerations to which team, in exchange for Matt Bruback, Jose Hernandez, and Bobby Hill?

a. Texas Rangers

b. Chicago Cubs

c. Milwaukee Brewers

d. Los Angeles Dodgers

10. The Pittsburgh Pirates have made 9 trades with the Florida/Miami Marlins all time (as of the end of the 2020 season).

a. True

b. False

11. On July 30, 2001, the Pittsburgh Pirates traded Jason Schmidt and John Vander Wal to which team, in exchange for Ryan Vogelsong and Armando Rios?

    a. Tampa Bay Devil Rays
    b. Toronto Blue Jays
    c. Arizona Diamondbacks
    d. San Francisco Giants

12. The Pittsburgh Pirates have made only 9 trades with the San Diego Padres all time.

    a. True
    b. False

13. How many trades have the Pittsburgh Pirates made with the Milwaukee Brewers all?

    a. 12
    b. 15
    c. 20
    d. 22

14. The Pittsburgh Pirates have made 16 trades with the Houston Astros all time.

    a. True
    b. False

15. On December 9, 1980, the Pittsburgh Pirates traded Bert Blyleven and Manny Sanguillen to which team, in exchange for Gary Alexander, Victor Cruz, Bob Owchinko, and Rafael Vasquez?

a. Oakland A's

b. California Angels

c. Cleveland Indians

d. Minnesota Twins

16. On December 11, 1975, the Pittsburgh Pirates traded Dock Ellis, Willie Randolph, and Ken Brett to which team, in exchange for Doc Medich?

a. Texas Rangers

b. New York Yankees

c. Seattle Mariners

d. New York Mets

17. On January 15, 2018, the Pittsburgh Pirates traded Andrew McCutchen and cash considerations to which team, in exchange for Kyle Crick, Bryan Reynolds, and international bonus slot money?

a. Oakland A's

b. New York Yankees

c. Philadelphia Phillies

d. San Francisco Giants

18. On July 31, 2018, the Pittsburgh Pirates traded Tyler Glasnow, Austin Meadows, and a player to be named later (Shane Baz) to which team, in exchange for Chris Archer?

a. Atlanta Braves

b. Toronto Blue Jays

c. Tampa Bay Rays

d. Washington Nationals

19. On August 2, 1985, the Pittsburgh Pirates traded George Hendrick, Al Holland, and which other player, to the California Angels in exchange for Mike Brown, Pat Clements. and a player to be named later (Bob Kipper)?

    a.  Jose DeLeon
    b.  John Candelaria
    c.  Cecilio Guante
    d.  Tim Foli

20. The Pittsburgh Pirates have made 11 trades with the Tampa Bay Rays/Devil Rays all.

    a.  True
    b.  False

# QUIZ ANSWERS

1. B – St. Louis Cardinals

2. C – Cincinnati Reds

3. A – True

4. D – Bobby Bonilla

5. A- True

6. C – New York Yankees

7. B – Cleveland Indians

8. C – San Diego Padres

9. B – Chicago Cubs

10. A- True

11. D – San Francisco Giants

12. B – False, 18

13. A – 12

14. A – True

15. C – Cleveland Indians

16. B – New York Yankees

17. D – San Francisco Giants

18. C – Tampa Bay Rays

19. B – John Candelaria

20. A- True

# DID YOU KNOW?

1. On November 27, 2004, the Pittsburgh Pirates traded Jason Kendall and cash considerations to the Oakland A's in exchange for Arthur Rhodes, Mark Redman, and cash considerations.

2. On June 4, 1953, the Pittsburgh Pirates traded Ralph Kiner, Joe Garagiola, George Metkovich, and Howie Pollet to the Chicago Cubs in exchange for Bob Addis, Toby Atwell, George Freese, Gene Hermanski, Bob Schultz, Preston Ward, and $150,000.

3. On December 10, 1965, the Pittsburgh Pirates traded Bob Friend to the New York Yankees in exchange for Pete Mikkelsen and cash considerations.

4. On January 13, 2018, the Pittsburgh Pirates traded Gerritt Cole to the Houston Astros in exchange for Michael Feliz, Jason Martin, Colin Moran, and Joe Musgrove.

5. On August 21, 2008, the Pittsburgh Pirates traded Jose Bautista to the Toronto Blue Jays in exchange for a player to be named later (Robinzon Diaz).

6. On February 19, 2012, the Pittsburgh Pirates traded Diego Moreno and Exicardo Cayones to the New York Yankees in exchange for A.J. Burnett and cash considerations.

7. On December 9, 2015, the Pittsburgh Pirates traded Neil Walker to the New York Mets in exchange for Jon Niese.

8. On July 31, 2001, the Pittsburgh Pirates traded Terry Mulholland to the Los Angeles Dodgers in exchange for Mike Fetters and Adrian Burnside.

9. The Pittsburgh Pirates have made 20 trades with the Los Angeles.

10. The Pittsburgh Pirates have made 18 trades with the Minnesota.

# CHAPTER 8:

# DRAFT DAY

## QUIZ TIME!

1. Dave Parker was drafted by the Pittsburgh Pirates in which round of the 1970 MLB Draft?

    a. 2nd

    b. 5th

    c. 10th

    d. 14th

2. John Candelaria was drafted by the Pittsburgh Pirates in which round of the 1972 MLB Draft?

    a. 2nd

    b. 3rd

    c. 14th

    d. 16th

3. With which overall pick in the 1st round of the 2001 MLB Draft, the Pittsburgh Pirates selected Barry Bonds?

    a. 1st

    b. 2nd

c. 6th

d. 9th

4. With which overall pick in the 1st round of the 2005 MLB Draft, the Pittsburgh Pirates selected Andrew McCutchen?

   a. 1st

   b. 3rd

   c. 11th

   d. 12th

5. In the 8th round of the 1995 MLB Draft, which team selected A.J. Burnett?

   a. Toronto Blue Jays

   b. New York Yankees

   c. Florida Marlins

   d. New York Mets

6. Andy Van Slyke was drafted by which team in the 1st round, 6th overall of the 1979 MLB Draft?

   a. Pittsburgh Pirates

   b. St. Louis Cardinals

   c. Philadelphia Phillies

   d. Baltimore Orioles

7. Jason Kendall was drafted by the Pittsburgh Pirates in the 1st round, 23rd overall in the 1992 MLB Draft.

   a. True

   b. False

8. With which overall pick in the 1$^{st}$ round of the 2004 MLB Draft, the Pittsburgh Pirates selected Neil Walker?

    a. 5$^{th}$

    b. 8$^{th}$

    c. 11$^{th}$

    d. 19$^{th}$

9. With which overall pick in the 1$^{st}$ round of the 2008 MLB Draft, the Pittsburgh Pirates selected Pedro Alvarez?

    a. 1$^{st}$

    b. 2$^{nd}$

    c. 16$^{th}$

    d. 20$^{th}$

10. Jordy Mercer was drafted by the Pittsburgh Pirates in the 3$^{rd}$ round of the 2008 MLB Draft.

    a. True

    b. False

11. With the 11$^{th}$ overall pick in the 1$^{st}$ round of the 2013 MLB Draft, which team selected Colin Moran?

    a. Oakland A's

    b. Miami Marlins

    c. Houston Astros

    d. Pittsburgh Pirates

12. Jose Bautista was drafted by the Pittsburgh Pirates in the 20$^{th}$ round of the 2000 MLB Draft.

    a. True

    b. False

13. Jason Bay was drafted by which team in the 22$^{nd}$ round of the 2000 MLB Draft?

    a.  Pittsburgh Pirates
    b.  San Diego Padres
    c.  Montreal Expos
    d.  New York Mets

14. Josh Harrison was drafted by which team in the 6$^{th}$ round of the 2008 MLB Draft?

    a.  Detroit Tigers
    b.  Pittsburgh Pirates
    c.  Washington Nationals
    d.  Chicago Cubs

15. David Freese was drafted by which team in the 9th round of the 2006 MLB Draft?

    a.  Los Angeles Angels
    b.  St. Louis Cardinals
    c.  San Diego Padres
    d.  Los Angeles Dodgers

16. Bronson Arroyo was drafted by the Pittsburgh Pirates in the what round of the 1995 MLB Draft?

    a.  2$^{nd}$
    b.  3$^{rd}$
    c.  9$^{th}$
    d.  10$^{th}$

17. With what overall pick in the 1$^{st}$ round of the 2011 MLB Draft, the Pittsburgh Pirates selected Gerrit Cole?

a.  1<sup>st</sup>

b.  2<sup>nd</sup>

c.  3<sup>rd</sup>

d.  4<sup>th</sup>

18. Kevin Young was drafted in the 7<sup>th</sup> round of MLB Draft by the Pittsburgh Pirates in what year?

   a.  1986

   b.  1989

   c.  1990

   d.  1993

19. With what overall pick in the 1<sup>st</sup> round of the 1971 MLB Draft, the Oakland A's selected Phil Garner?

   a.  1<sup>st</sup>

   b.  3<sup>rd</sup>

   c.  5<sup>th</sup>

   d.  7<sup>th</sup>

20. Bert Blyleven was drafted by the Minnesota Twins in the 3<sup>rd</sup> round of the 1969 MLB Draft.

   a.  True

   b.  False

# QUIZ ANSWERS

1.  D – 14$^{th}$

2.  A – 2$^{nd}$

3.  C – 6$^{th}$

4.  C – 11$^{th}$

5.  D – New York Mets

6.  B – St. Louis Cardinals

7.  A – True

8.  C – 11$^{th}$

9.  B – 2$^{nd}$

10. A – True

11. B – Miami Marlins

12. A – True

13. C – Montreal Expos

14. D – Chicago Cubs

15. C – San Diego Padres

16. B – 3$^{rd}$

17. A – 1$^{st}$

18. C – 1990

19. B – 3$^{rd}$

20. A – True

# DID YOU KNOW?

1.  Charlie Morton was drafted in the 3rd round of the 2002 MLB Draft by the Atlanta Braves.

2.  Mike Easler was drafted in the 14th round in the 1969 MLB Draft by the Houston Astros.

3.  Bill Madlock was drafted in the 5th round of the 1970 MLB Draft by the Washington Senators.

4.  Jason Schmidt was drafted in the 8th round of the 1991 MLB Draft by the Atlanta Braves.

5.  Ryan Vogelsong was drafted in the 5th round of the 1998 MLB Draft by the San Francisco Giants.

6.  Jack Wilson was drafted in the 9th round of the 1998 MLB Draft by the St. Louis Cardinals.

7.  Mark Melancon was drafted in the 9th round of the 2006 MLB Draft by the New York Yankees.

8.  Jason Grilli was drafted in the 1st round (4th overall) of the 1997 MLB Draft by the San Francisco Giants.

9.  Bryan Reynolds was drafted in the 2nd round of the 2016 MLB Draft by the San Francisco Giants.

10. Adam Frazier was drafted in the 6th round of the 2013 MLB Draft by the Pittsburgh Pirates.

# CHAPTER 9:

# ODDS & ENDS

## QUIZ TIME!

1. David Ross was the first MLB contestant on which show?

    a. Celebrity Masterchef

    b. Celebrity Big Brother

    c. Rupaul's Celebrity Drag Race

    d. Dancing with the Stars

2. Dale Sveum is the cousin of former Toronto Blue Jays player, John Olreud.

    a. True

    b. False

3. Andrew McCutchen proposed to his longtime girlfriend, Maria on which talk show?

    a. The Tonight Show with Jimmy Fallon

    b. The Late Late Show with James Corden

    c. The Ellen Degeneres Show

    d. The View

4. Early in his career, A.J. Burnett named his bats after songs by which artist(s)?

   a. Panic! at the Disco
   b. Marilyn Manson
   c. Madonna
   d. Michael Jackson

5. What is the name of Bronson Arroyo's 2005 debut album?

   a. *Rockin with Bronson*
   b. *Life's a Grand Slam*
   c. *Covering the Bases*
   d. *Another Day, Another Strikeout*

6. Gerrit Cole is the brother-in-law of which San Francisco Giants player?

   a. Buster Posey
   b. Brandon Crawford
   c. Brandon Belt
   d. Evan Longoria

7. Former Pirates Sean Casey and Dan Plesac are currently analysts on MLB Network.

   a. True
   b. False

8. Jason Kendall authored a book entitled: Throwback: A Big-League Catcher Tells How the Game Is Really Played, released in May of 2014.

   a. True
   b. False

9. Bert Blyleven played himself in which film?

   a. Back to the Future Part III
   b. Taking Care of Business
   c. Edward Scissorhands
   d. The Rookie

10. Which former Pirate coached the American League in the 2010 'Taco Bell All-Star Legends & Celebrity Softball Game'?

   a. Dave Parker
   b. Goose Gossage
   c. Andy Van Slyke
   d. Jason Kendall

11. Which famous singer once owned 25% of the Pittsburgh Pirates?

   a. Frank Sinatra
   b. Bing Crosby
   c. Bob Hope
   d. Tony Bennett

12. Bob Friend's son, Bob Friend Jr. was a professional golfer who played on the PGA Tour.

   a. True
   b. False

13. Bill Mazeroski made a cameo in which film?

   a. Planet of the Apes
   b. Once Upon a Time in the West

c.  The Odd Couple

d.  Funny Girl

14. Andy Van Slyke's son, Scott Van Slyke played for the Los Angeles Dodgers.

a.  True

b.  False

15. Jason Bay's sister, Lauren is a professional player in which sport?

a.  Basketball

b.  Tennis

c.  Soccer

d.  Softball

16. Doug Drabek's son, Kyle was a starting pitcher in the MLB who played for the Arizona Diamondbacks, Toronto Blue Jays and Chicago White Sox.

a.  True

b.  False

17. After his baseball career ended, what job did Babe Adams have during World War II and the Korean War?

a.  Factory Worker

b.  Reporter

c.  Landscaper

d.  Car Mechanic

18. In 2019, how much did a Honus Wagner T-206 baseball card sell for?

a. $657,000

b. $850,000

c. $1.2 Million

d. $2.1 Million

19. Tim Wakefield is one of the subjects of which baseball documentary?

a. Knuckleball

b. Ballplayer: Pelotero

c. Catching Hell

d. Long Shot

20. A species of weevil, Sicoderus bautistai, was named after Jose Bautsita in 2018.

a. True

b. False

# QUIZ ANSWERS

1. D – Dancing with the Stars

2. A – True

3. C – The Ellen DeGeneres Show

4. B – Marilyn Manson

5. C – *Covering the Bases*

6. B – Brandon Crawford

7. A – True

8. A – True

9. B – *Taking Care of Business*

10. B – Goose Gossage

11. B – Bing Crosby

12. A – True

13. C – *The Odd Couple*

14. A – True

15. D – Softball

16. A – True

17. B – Reporter

18. C - $1.2 Million

19. A – *Knuckleball*

20. A – True

# DID YOU KNOW?

1. Former Pirate, Dan Plesac has a nephew, Zach who currently pitches for the Cleveland Indians.

2. On February 4, 2015, Matt Stairs was elected to the Canadian Baseball Hall of Fame.

3. The New York Mets will be paying Bobby Bonilla over $1 million every July 1st until 2035. By the end of the deal, Bonilla will have been paid $29.8 million for a season in which he did not even play for the Mets. Many Mets and baseball fans refer to July 1st as "Bobby Bonilla Day".

4. Manny Sanguillen runs a BBQ concession stand at PNC Park called "Manny's BBQ". He likes to sit at the stand and sign autographs, take pictures and greet fans.

5. Moises Alou did not wear batting gloves. He claims he would urinate on his hands to make them tougher.

6. Pedro Alvarez's wife, Keli is the daughter of former San Diego Padres manager, Pat Murphy.

7. Jason Grilli's father, Steve pitched in the MLB as well, playing for the Detroit Tigers and Toronto Blue Jays.

8. Francisco Liriano is cousins with fellow former MLB pitcher, Santiago Casilla.

9. Mark Melancon was a member of the National Honor Society in high school.

10. Mike Easler is an ordained Baptist minister.

# CHAPTER 10:

# OUTFIELDERS

## QUIZ TIME!

1. How many MLB All-Star Games was Roberto Clemente named to over the course of his 18-season MLB career?

   a. 10

   b. 12

   c. 15

   d. 18

2. Willie Stargell was inducted into the National Baseball Hall of Fame in 1988.

   a. True

   b. False

3. What year was Paul Waner inducted into the National Baseball Hall of Fame?

   a. 1950

   b. 1952

   c. 1954

   d. 1956

4. Ralph Kiner spent his entire 10-season career with the Pittsburgh Pirates.

   a. True

   b. False

5. As of the end of the 2020 season, how many Silver Slugger Awards does Andrew McCutchen have?

   a. 1

   b. 2

   c. 3

   d. 4

6. How many Gold Glove Awards did Barry Bonds win over the course of his 22-season MLB career?

   a. 5

   b. 8

   c. 9

   d. 10

7. Dave Parker played 11 seasons with the Pittsburgh Pirates.

   a. True

   b. False

8. Over the course of his 10-season MLB career, Starling Marte played for the Pittsburgh Pirates, Arizona Diamondbacks, and which other team?

   a. Chicago Cubs

   b. St. Louis Cardinals

c.  Miami Marlins

d.  Los Angeles Dodgers

9. How many seasons did Nate McClouth spend with the Pittsburgh Pirates?

a.  3

b.  4

c.  6

d.  8

10. How many MLB All-Star Games was Jason Bay named to over the course of his 11-season MLB career?

a.  1

b.  2

c.  3

d.  4

11. How many Gold Glove Awards did Andy Van Slyke win over the course of his 13-season MLB career?

a.  2

b.  3

c.  5

d.  6

12. Al Oliver spent 10 seasons of his MLB career with the Pittsburgh Pirates.

a.  True

b.  False

13. What year did Matty Alou win the NL Batting Title?

a.  1966

b.  1967

c.  1968

d.  1969

14. Bill Virdon spent 11 years of his MLB career with the Pittsburgh Pirates and 2 years with which team?

a.  New York Yankees

b.  Texas Rangers

c.  Cincinnati Reds

d.  St. Louis Cardinals

15. How many MLB All-Star Games was Bob Skinner named to over the course of his 12-season MLB career?

a.  0

b.  1

c.  2

d.  3

16. 16. How many Silver Slugger Awards did Bobby Bonilla win over the course of his 16-season MLB career?

a.  1

b.  2

c.  3

d.  4

17. How many MLB All-Star Games was Richie Zisk named to over the course of his 13-season MLB career?

a.  1

b.  2

c.  4

d.  5

18. How many seasons did Omar Moreno spend with the Pittsburgh Pirates?

    a.  3

    b.  4

    c.  7

    d.  8

19. How many MLB All-Star Games was Lee Mazzilli named to over the course of his 14-season MLB career?

    a.  0

    b.  1

    c.  2

    d.  3

20. Jerry Lynch spent 7 seasons of his MLB career with the Pittsburgh Pirates and 7 seasons with the Cincinnati Reds.

    a.  True

    b.  False

# QUIZ ANSWERS

1. C – 15

2. A – True

3. B – 1952

4. B – False, Pirates, Chicago Cubs and Cleveland Indians

5. D – 4

6. B – 8

7. A – True

8. C – Miami Marlins

9. C – 6

10. C – 3

11. C – 5

12. A – True

13. A – 1966

14. D – St. Louis Cardinals

15. D – 3

16. C – 3

17. B – 2

18. D – 8

19. B – 1

20. A – True

# DID YOU KNOW?

1. Roberto Clemente spent his entire 18-season MLB career with the Pittsburgh Pirates. He is a member of the National Baseball Hall of Fame, MVP, 15x MLB All-Star, 12x Gold Glove Award winner, 2x World Series Champion, World Series MVP, and 4x Batting Title Champion.

2. Willie Stargell spent his entire 21-season MLB career with the Pittsburgh Pirates. He is a member of the National Baseball Hall of Fame, MVP, 7x MLB All-Star, 2x World Series Champion, World Series MVP NLCS MVP, and Major League Player of the Year.

3. Paul Waner spent 15 seasons of his MLB career with the Pittsburgh Pirates. He also played for the Brooklyn Dodgers, New York Yankees, and Boston Braves. He is a member of the National Baseball Hall of Fame, MVP, 4x MLB All-Star and 3x Batting Title Champion.

4. Dave Parker spent 11 seasons of his MLB career with the Pittsburgh Pirates. He also played for the Cincinnati Reds, Oakland A's, California Angels, Toronto Blue Jays and Milwaukee Brewers. He is a MVP, 7x MLB All-Star, 2x World Series Champion, 3x Gold Glove Award winner, 3x Silver Slugger Award winner, 2x Batting Title Champion, and All-Star Game MVP.

5.  Barry Bonds spent 7 seasons of his MLB career with the Pittsburgh Pirates. He also played for the San Francisco Giants. He is a 7x MVP, 14x MLB All-Star, 8x Gold Glove Award winner, 12x Silver Slugger Award winner, 2x Batting Title Champion, and 3x Major League Player of the Year.

6.  Ralph Kiner spent 8 seasons of his MLB career with the Pittsburgh Pirates. He also played for the Chicago Cubs and Cleveland Indians. He is a member of the National Baseball Hall of Fame and 6x MLB All-Star.

7.  Andrew McCutchen spent 9 seasons of his MLB career with the Pittsburgh Pirates, he currently plays across the state for the Philadelphia Phillies. He has also played for the New York Yankees, and San Francisco Giants. As of the end of the 2020 season, he is an MVP, Gold Glove Award winner, 5x MLB All-Star, and 4x Silver Slugger Award winner.

8.  Starling Marte spent 8 seasons of his MLB career with the Pittsburgh Pirates, he has also played for the Arizona Diamondbacks and is currently playing with the Miami Marlins. He is an MLB All-Star and 2x Gold Glove Award winner.

9.  Al Oliver spent 10 seasons of his MLB career with the Pittsburgh Pirates. He also played for the Texas Rangers, Montreal Expos, Los Angeles Dodgers, San Francisco Giants, Philadelphia Phillies, and Toronto Blue Jays. He is

a 7x MLB All-Star, 3x Silver Slugger Award winner, Batting Title Champion, and World Series Champion.

10. Bill Virdon spent 11 seasons of his MLB career with the Pittsburgh Pirates. He also played for the St. Louis Cardinals. He is a NL Rookie of the Year Award winner, Gold Glove Award winner, and World Series Champion.

# CHAPTER 11:

# INFIELDERS

## QUIZ TIME!

1. What year was Pie Traynor inducted into the National Baseball Hall of Fame?

    a. 1942
    b. 1945
    c. 1948
    d. 1950

2. Bill Mazeroski spent his entire 17-season MLB career with the Pittsburgh Pirates.

    a. True
    b. False

3. How many seasons did Jay Bell spend with the Pittsburgh Pirates?

    a. 2
    b. 4
    c. 6
    d. 8

4. How many National League Batting Titles did Bill Madlock win over the course of his 15-season MLB career?

    a. 1
    b. 2
    c. 3
    d. 4

5. How many MLB All-Star Games was Aramis Ramirez named to over the course of his 18-season MLB career?

    a. 1
    b. 3
    c. 4
    d. 6

6. How many MLB All-Star Games was Freddy Sanchez named to over the course of his 10-season MLB career?

    a. 1
    b. 2
    c. 3
    d. 4

7. Adam LaRoche and his brother, Andy LaRoche both played for the Pittsburgh Pirates.

    a. True
    b. False

8. How many Silver Slugger Awards did Jose Bautista win over the course of his 15-season MLB career?

a. 0

b. 1

c. 2

d. 3

9. Rafael Belliard spent 9 seasons of his MLB career with the Pittsburgh Pirates and 8 seasons with which team?

   a. Houston Astros

   b. Atlanta Braves

   c. Kansas City Royals

   d. Tampa Bay Rays

10. How many MLB All-Star Games was Phil Garner named to over the course of his 16-season MLB career?

    a. 1

    b. 2

    c. 3

    d. 4

11. How many seasons did Richie Hebner spend with the Pittsburgh Pirates?

    a. 9

    b. 11

    c. 13

    d. 15

12. Rennie Stennett spent 9 seasons of his MLB career with the Pittsburgh Pirates and 2 seasons with the San Francisco Giants.

    a. True

    b. False

13. How many seasons did Don Clendenon spend with the Pittsburgh Pirates?

    a.  7
    b.  8
    c.  9
    d.  10

14. How many MLB All-Star Games was Maury Wills named to over the course of his 14-season MLB career?

    a.  3
    b.  4
    c.  5
    d.  7

15. How many MLB All-Star Games was Dick Stuart named to over the course of his 10-season MLB career?

    a.  0
    b.  1
    c.  2
    d.  3

16. Gene Alley spent his entire 11-season MLB career with the Pittsburgh Pirates.

    a.  True
    b.  False

17. How many MLB All-Star Games was David Freese named to over the course of his 11-season MLB career?

    a.  0
    b.  1

c. 2

d. 3

18. How many MLB All-Star Games was Ted Kluszewski named to over the course of his 15-season MLB career?

    a. 2

    b. 3

    c. 4

    d. 6

19. How many MLB All-Star Games was Frank Thomas named to over the course of his 16-season MLB career?

    a. 0

    b. 1

    c. 2

    d. 3

20. Dick Groat missed the 1953 and 1954 seasons due to military service.

    a. True

    b. False

# QUIZ ANSWERS

1. C – 1948

2. A- True

3. D – 8

4. D – 4

5. B – 3

6. C – 3

7. A – True

8. D – 3

9. B – Atlanta Braves

10. C – 3

11. B – 11

12. A – True

13. B – 8

14. D – 7

15. C – 2

16. A – True

17. B – 1

18. C – 4

19. D – 3

20. A – True

# DID YOU KNOW?

1. Bill Mazeroski spent his entire 17-season MLB career with the Pittsburgh Pirates. He is a member of the National Baseball Hall of Fame, 10x MLB All-Star, 8x Gold Glove Award winner, 2x World Series Champion, and Major League Player of the Year.

2. Pie Traynor spent his entire 17-season MLB career with the Pittsburgh Pirates. He is a member of the National Baseball Hall of Fame, 2x MLB All-Star, and World Series Champion.

3. Jay Bell spent 8 seasons of his MLB career with the Pittsburgh Pirates. He also played for the Arizona Diamondbacks, Cleveland Indians, Kansas City Royals, and New York Mets. He is a 2x MLB All-Star, Gold Glove Award winner, World Series Champion, and Silver Slugger Award winner.

4. Bill Madlock spent 7 seasons of his MLB career with the Pittsburgh Pirates. He also played for the Los Angeles Dodgers, Chicago Cubs, San Francisco Giants, Texas Rangers, and Detroit Tigers. He is a 3x MLB All-Star, World Series Champion, 4x Batting Title Champion and All-Star Game MVP.

5. Jose Bautista spent 5 seasons of his MLB career with the Pittsburgh Pirates. He also played for the Toronto Blue

Jays, Kansas City Royals, New York Mets, Tampa Bay Devil Rays, Philadelphia Phillies, Atlanta Braves and Baltimore Orioles. He is a 6x MLB All-Star and 3x Silver Slugger Award winner.

6. David Freese spent 3 seasons of his MLB career with the Pittsburgh Pirates. He also played for the St. Louis Cardinals, Los Angeles Dodgers, and Los Angeles Angels. He is a 1x MLB All-Star, World Series Champion, World Series MVP, and NLCS MVP.

7. Gene Alley spent his entire 11-season MLB career with the Pittsburgh Pirates. He is a 2x MLB All-Star, 2x Gold Glove Award winner, and World Series Champion.

8. Maury Wills spent 2 seasons of his MLB career with the Pittsburgh Pirates. He also played for the Los Angeles Dodgers and Montreal Expos. He is an MVP, 7x MLB All-Star, 3x World Series Champion, 2x Gold Glove Award winner, All-Star MVP, and Major League Player of the Year.

9. Ted Kluszewski spent 2 seasons of his MLB career with the Pittsburgh Pirates. He also played for the Chicago White Sox and Los Angeles Angels. He is a 4x MLB All-Star.

10. Richie Hebner spent 11 seasons of his MLB career with the Pittsburgh Pirates. He also played for the Detroit Tigers, Chicago Cubs, Philadelphia Phillies, and New York Mets. He is a 1971 World Series Champion.

# CHAPTER 12:

# PITCHERS AND CATCHERS

## QUIZ TIME!

1. How many MLB All-Star Games was Jason Kendall named to over the course of his 15-season MLB career?

    a. 2

    b. 3

    c. 4

    d. 5

2. Babe Adams spent 18 seasons with the Pittsburgh Pirates.

    a. True

    b. False

3. How many MLB All-Star Games was Bob Friend named to over the course of his 16-season MLB career?

    a. 1

    b. 2

    c. 3

    d. 4

4. What year did John Candelaria win the NL Pitching Title?

    a. 1976
    b. 1977
    c. 1978
    d. 1979

5. Ryan Vogelsong spent 6 seasons of his MLB career with the Pittsburgh Pirates and 7 seasons with which team?

    a. Texas Rangers
    b. Chicago White Sox
    c. Arizona Diamondbacks
    d. San Francisco Giants

6. Manny Sanguillén spent 12 seasons of his MLB career with the Pittsburgh Pirates and 1 season with which team?

    a. Milwaukee Brewers
    b. Los Angeles Dodgers
    c. Oakland A's
    d. Chicago Cubs

7. Vern Law spent his entire 16-season MLB career with the Pittsburgh Pirates.

    a. True
    b. False

8. What year did Doug Drabek win a Cy Young Award?

    a. 1935
    b. 1988

c. 1990

d. 1991

9. How many MLB All-Star Games was Russell Martin named to over the course of his 14-season MLB career?

    a. 1

    b. 2

    c. 3

    d. 4

10. How many Gold Glove Awards did Tony Peña win over the course of his 18-season MLB career?

    a. 2

    b. 4

    c. 6

    d. 8

11. What year was Goose Gossage inducted into the National Baseball Hall of Fame?

    a. 2006

    b. 2007

    c. 2008

    d. 2009

12. Bert Blyleven was not inducted into the National Baseball Hall of Fame until 2011.

    a. True

    b. False

13. How many seasons did A.J. Burnett spend with the Pittsburgh Pirates?

    a.  2
    b.  3
    c.  5
    d.  6

14. Tim Wakefield spent 2 seasons of his MLB career with the Pittsburgh Pirates and 17 seasons with which team?

    a.  New York Yankees
    b.  Atlanta Braves
    c.  Cincinnati Reds
    d.  Boston Red Sox

15. How many MLB All-Star Games was Dan Plesac named to over the course of his 18-season MLB career?

    a.  1
    b.  2
    c.  3
    d.  4

16. Ryan Doumit spent 7 seasons of his MLB career with the Pittsburgh Pirates.

    a.  True
    b.  False

17. How many MLB All-Star Games was Jason Schmidt named to over the course of his 14-season MLB career?

    a.  0
    b.  1

c. 2

d. 3

18. How many Gold Glove Awards did Mike LaValliere win over the course of his 12-season MLB career?

    a. 0

    b. 1

    c. 2

    d. 3

19. How many seasons did Roy Face spend with the Pittsburgh Pirates?

    a. 5

    b. 10

    c. 15

    d. 20

20. Don Slaught spent 6 seasons with the Pittsburgh Pirates.

    a. True

    b. False

# QUIZ ANSWERS

1. B – 3

2. A – True

3. D – 4

4. B – 1977

5. D – San Francisco Giants

6. C – Oakland A's

7. A – True

8. C – 1990

9. D – 4

10. B – 4

11. C – 2008

12. A – True

13. B – 3

14. D – Boston Red Sox

15. C – 3

16. A – True

17. D – 3

18. B – 1

19. C – 15

20. A – True

# DID YOU KNOW?

1. Jason Kendall spent 9 seasons of his MLB career with the Pittsburgh Pirates. He also played for the Oakland A's, Milwaukee Brewers, Kansas City Royals, and Chicago Cubs. He is a 3x MLB All-Star.

2. Vern Law spent his entire 16-season MLB career with the Pittsburgh Pirates. He is a Cy Young Award winner, 2x MLB All-Star, and 1960 World Series Champion.

3. Bob Friend spent 15 seasons of his MLB career with the Pittsburgh Pirates. He also played for the New York Mets and New York Yankees. He is a 4x MLB All-Star, NL Pitching Title Champion, and 1960 World Series Champion.

4. Manny Sanguillén spent 12 seasons of his MLB career with the Pittsburgh Pirates. He also played for the Oakland A's. He is a 3x MLB All-Star and 2x World Series Champion.

5. Bert Blyleven spent 3 seasons of his MLB career with the Pittsburgh Pirates. He also played for the Minnesota Twins, Cleveland Indians, California Angels, and Texas Rangers. He is a member of the National Baseball Hall of Fame, 2x MLB All-Star, and 2x World Series Champion.

6. Tony Peña spent 7 seasons of his MLB career with the Pittsburgh Pirates. He also played for the Boston Red Sox, Cleveland Indians, St. Louis Cardinals, Houston Astros

and Chicago White Sox. He is a 5x MLB All-Star and 4x Gold Glove Award winner.

7. John Candelaria spent 12 seasons of his MLB career with the Pittsburgh Pirates. He also played for the California Angels, Los Angeles Dodgers, New York Yankees, Minnesota Twins, New York Mets, Montreal Expos, and Toronto Blue Jays. He is an MLB All-Star, NL Pitching Title champion and 1979 World Series Champion.

8. Ryan Vogelsong spent 6 seasons of his MLB career with the Pittsburgh Pirates. He also played for the San Francisco Giants. He is an MLB All-Star and 2x World Series Champion.

9. Roy Face spent 15 seasons of his MLB career with the Pittsburgh Pirates. He also played for the Montreal Expos and Detroit Tigers. He is a 6x MLB All-Star and 1960 World Series Champion.

10. Jason Schmidt spent 6 seasons of his MLB career with the Pittsburgh Pirates. He also played for the San Francisco Giants, Atlanta Braves and Los Angeles Dodgers. He is a 3x MLB All-Star and NL Pitching Title champion.

# CHAPTER 13:

# WORLD SERIES

## QUIZ TIME!

1. How many World Series Championships have the Pittsburgh Pirates won in franchise history?

    a. 1
    b. 3
    c. 5
    d. 7

2. How many NL Pennants have the Pittsburgh Pirates won (as of the end of the 2020 season)?

    a. 5
    b. 6
    c. 8
    d. 9

3. Which team did the Pittsburgh Pirates face in the 1903 World Series?

    a. Chicago White Stockings
    b. Philadelphia Athletics

c. Boston Americans

d. New York Highlanders

4. Which team did the Pittsburgh Pirates face in the 1909 World Series?

   a. Philadelphia Athletics

   b. Detroit Tigers

   c. Cleveland Naps

   d. St. Louis Browns

5. Which team did the Pittsburgh Pirates face in the 1925 World Series?

   a. Washington Senators

   b. Philadelphia Athletics

   c. St. Louis Browns

   d. Detroit Tigers

6. Which team did the Pittsburgh Pirates face in the 1927 World Series?

   a. Philadelphia Athletics

   b. New York Yankees

   c. Boston Red Sox

   d. Washington Senators

7. The Pittsburgh Pirates faced the New York Yankees in the 1960 World Series.

   a. True

   b. False

8. Which team did the Pittsburgh Pirates face in the 1971 World Series?

a. Oakland A's

b. California Angels

c. Baltimore Orioles

d. Kansas City Royals

9. Which team did the Pittsburgh Pirates face in the 1979 World Series?

    a. Oakland A's

    b. California Angels

    c. Baltimore Orioles

    d. Kansas City Royals

10. What year did the Pittsburgh Pirates NOT win a Wild Card berth?

    a. 2012

    b. 2013

    c. 2014

    d. 2015

11. How many games did the 1903 World Series go?

    a. 5

    b. 6

    c. 7

    d. 8

12. The 1909 World Series went 7 games.

    a. True

    b. False

13. How many games did the 1925 World Series go?

a. 4

b. 5

c. 6

d. 7

14. How many games did the 1927 World Series go?

a. 4

b. 5

c. 6

d. 7

15. How many games did the 1960 World Series go?

a. 4

b. 5

c. 6

d. 7

16. The 1971 World Series went 7 games.

a. True

b. False

17. How many games did the 1979 World Series go?

a. 4

b. 5

c. 6

d. 7

18. Who was the manager of the Pittsburgh Pirates during the 1903 and 1909 World Series?

a. Honus Wagner

b. Fred Clarke

c. Bill McKechnie

d. Bill Watkins

19. Who was manager of the Pittsburgh Pirates during the 1925 World Series'?

    a. Pie Traynor

    b. Donie Bush

    c. Bill McKechnie

    d. Spud Davis

20. Donie Bush was manager of the Pittsburgh Pirates during the 1927 World Series.

    a. True

    b. False

# QUIZ ANSWERS

1.  C – 5 (1909, 1925, 1960, 1971, 1979)

2.  D – 9 (1901, 1902, 1903, 1909, 1925, 1927, 1960, 1971, 1979)

3.  C – Boston Americans

4.  B – Detroit Tigers

5.  A – Washington Senators

6.  B – New York Yankees

7.  A – True

8.  C – Baltimore Orioles

9.  C – Baltimore Orioles

10. A – 2012

11. D – 8

12. A - True

13. D – 7

14. A – 4

15. D – 7

16. A – True

17. D – 7

18. B – Fred Clarke

19. C – Bill McKechnie

20. A – True

# DID YOU KNOW?

1. Danny Murtaugh was manager of the Pittsburgh Pirates during the 1960 and 1971 World Series.

2. Chuck Tanner was manager of the Pittsburgh Pirates during the 1979 World Series.

3. The Pittsburgh Pirates won the NL Pennant in 1901 and 1902. The first World Series did not take place until 1903.

4. The Pittsburgh Pirates participated in the first World Series in MLB history. In 1903 they faced the Boston Americans.

5. Although the Pittsburgh Pirates won the 1960 World Series, Bobby Richardson of the New York Yankees was named MVP. This was the only time in MLB history that the MVP Award was given to a member of the losing team.

6. The 1970 World Series MVP was Roberto Clemente. The 1979 World Series MVP was Willie Stargell.

7. The 1903 World Series took place from October 1 – October 13. The 1909 World Series took place from October 8 – October 16. The 1925 World Series took place from October 7 – October 15. The 1927 World Series took place from October 5 – October 8. The 1960 World Series took place from October 5 – October 13. The 1971 World

Series took place from October 9 – October 17. The 1979 World Series took place from October 10 – October 17.

8.  The 1979 Pittsburgh Pirates were the last team to win a World Series Game 7 on the road until the San Francisco Giants in 2014.

9.  The 1971 World Series was the first of three consecutive World Series' where the winning team scored fewer runs overall than the losing team.

10. The 1960 World Series is the most recent Pittsburgh sports championship to be won at home.

# CHAPTER 14:

# HEATED RIVALRIES

## QUIZ TIME!

1. Which team does NOT play in the National League Central with the Pittsburgh Pirates?

   a. Chicago White Sox
   b. Chicago Cubs
   c. Cincinnati Reds
   d. Detroit Tigers

2. The Pittsburgh Pirates were a part of the National League East Division from 1969-1993.

   a. True
   b. False

3. Which team below was once a member of the NL Central Division?

   a. Philadelphia Phillies
   b. Houston Astros
   c. Chicago White Sox
   d. Minnesota Twins

4.  What current National League Central team has the most NL Central Championships?

    a.  Milwaukee Brewers
    b.  Chicago Cubs
    c.  Cincinnati Reds
    d.  St. Louis Cardinals

5.  From 1998-2013 the NL Central was the MLB's largest division.

    a.  True
    b.  False

6.  Which team won the National League Central in 2020?

    a.  St. Louis Cardinals
    b.  Chicago Cubs
    c.  Cincinnati Reds
    d.  Detroit Tigers

7.  The Pittsburgh Pirates have never won a NL Central Division Championship.

    a.  True
    b.  False

8.  How many World Series Championships do the St. Louis Cardinals have?

    a.  5
    b.  6
    c.  11
    d.  12

9. How many World Series Championships do the Chicago Cubs have?

    a. 0

    b. 1

    c. 2

    d. 3

10. How many World Series Championships do the Cincinnati Reds have?

    a. 1

    b. 2

    c. 5

    d. 6

11. How many World Series Championships do the Milwaukee Brewers have?

    a. 0

    b. 1

    c. 2

    d. 43

12. The Philadelphia Phillies have won 2 World Series Championships.

    a. True

    b. False

13. Which player has NOT played for both the Pittsburgh Pirates and the St. Louis Cardinals?

    a. Babe Adams

    b. Bobby Bonilla

c. Andy Van Slyke

d. Jason Kendall

14. Which player has NOT played for both the Pittsburgh Pirates and the Milwaukee Brewers?

    a. Jason Kendall

    b. Brian Giles

    c. Dave Parker

    d. Neil Walker

15. Which player has NOT played for both the Pittsburgh Pirates and the Cincinnati Reds?

    a. Bronson Arroyo

    b. Ted Kluszewski

    c. Kevin Young

    d. David Ross

16. The National League Central division was founded in 1994.

    a. True

    b. False

17. Which player has NOT played for both the Pittsburgh Pirates and the Chicago Cubs?

    a. Goose Gossage

    b. Jason Bay

    c. Ralph Kiner

    d. Kenny Lofton

18. Which player has NOT played for both the Pittsburgh Pirates and the Philadelphia Phillies?

    a. Jose Bautista
    b. A.J. Burnett
    c. Xavier Nady
    d. Mike Easler

19. How many NL Central Division titles did the Houston Astros win before they moved to the AL West?

    a. 0
    b. 1
    c. 3
    d. 4

20. The Pittsburgh Pirates won 9 NL East division championships before they moved to the NL Central.

    a. True
    b. False

# QUIZ ANSWERS

1.  D – Detroit Tigers

2.  A – True

3.  B – Houston Astros

4.  D – St. Louis Cardinals (11)

5.  A – True

6.  B – Chicago Cubs

7.  A – True

8.  C – 11

9.  D – 3

10. C – 5

11. A – 0

12. A – True

13. D – Jason Kendall

14. B – Brian Giles

15. C – Kevin Young

16. A- True

17. B – Jason Bay

18. C – Xavier Nady

19. D – 4

20. A – True

# DID YOU KNOW?

1. The St. Louis Cardinals have the most National League Central Division Championships with 11 total. The Chicago Cubs have 6, the Cincinnati Reds have 3, the Milwaukee Brewers have 2, and the Pittsburgh Pirates have 0. The Houston Astros formerly of the NL Central, won 4 division championships during their time in the NL Central. The Pittsburgh Pirates won 9 NL East Championships (1970, 1971, 1972, 1974, 1975, 1979, 1990, 1991, 1992). The most recent NL Central Division Champions are the Chicago Cubs (2020).

2. When the NL Central was founded, the Pirates were originally supposed to stay in the NL East with the Atlanta Braves set to move to the NL Central from the NL West. The Braves requested to stay in the East division due to their rivalry with the Florida Marlins. The Pirates have requested to be placed back in the East division several times.

3. The Chicago Cubs, Cincinnati Reds, St. Louis Cardinals, Houston Astros, and Pittsburgh Pirates are all founding members of the National League Central Division.

4. The first NL Central Division Champions were the Cincinnati Reds in 1995. There were no playoffs in 1994 due to an MLB strike.

5. The Milwaukee Brewers are the only team in the National League Central who have NOT won a World Series Championship.

6. Babe Adams, Matty Alou, John Axford, Bobby Bonilla, Donn Clendenon, Spud Davis, Octavio Dotel, Davis Freese, Gene Freese, Mudcat Grant, Dick Groat, Harvey Haddix, Brian Harper, Art Howe, Ron Kline, Mike LaValliere, Ryan Ludwick, Gene Mauch, Charlie Morton, Brandon Moss, Johnny O'Brien, Tony Pena, Jerry Reuss, Ricardo Rincon, Reggie Sanders, Dick Schofield, Bob Skinner, Lonnie Smith, Jake Stenzel, Andy Van Slyke, Bill Virdon, Rick White, Ty Wiggington, and Tony Womack have all played for both the Pittsburgh Pirates and the St. Louis Cardinals.

7. Moises Alou, Smoky Burgess, Ronny Cedeno, Dave Clark, Wilbur Cooper, Goose Gossage, Richie Hebner, Don Hoak, Derek Holland, Jason Kendall, Ralph Kiner, Tommy Leach, Kenny Lofton, Dale Long, Bill Madlock, Pat Mahomes, Gary Matthews, Lloyd McClendon, Casey McGehee, Terry Mulholland, Xavier Nady, Dan Plesac, Aramis Ramirez, Dave Roberts, David Ross, Matt Stairs, Jake Stenzel, Frank Thomas, Daryle Ward, and Tony Womack have all played for both the Pittsburgh Pirates and the Chicago Cubs.

8. Cal Abrams, Bronson Arroyo, Bob Bailey, Bo Belinsky, Gus Bell, Smoky Burgess, Marlon Byrd, Sean Casey, Spud Davis, Vince DiMaggio, Gene Freese, Johnny Gooch, Jose

Guillen, Harvey Haddix, Don Hoak, Brian Hunter Ted Kluszewski, Tommy Leach, Red Lucas, Ryan Ludwick, Jerry Lynch, Carmelo Martinez, Ross Ohlendorf, Joe Oliver, Dave Parker, Joe Randa, Pokey Reese, David Ross, Reggie Sanders, Benito Santiago, Bob Skinner, Jake Stenzel, Jesse Tannehill, Frank Thomas, Bobby Tolan, John Vander Wal, Rick White, and Tony Womack have all played for both the Pittsburgh Pirates and the Cincinnati Reds.

9. John Axford, Chris Duffy, Brian Harper, Jason Kendall, Casey McGehee, Nyjer Morgan, Lyle Overbay, Dave Parker, Dan Plesac, Aramis Ramirez, Dick Schofield, Joakim Soria, Matt Stairs, Dale Sveum, John Vander Wal, and Neil Walker have all played for both the Pittsburgh Pirates and the Milwaukee Brewers.

10. Bill Almon, Rod Barajas, Jose Bautista, Bo Belinsky, Joe Blanton, Smoky Burgess, A.J. Burnett, Marlon Byrd, Ronny Cedeno, Spud Davis, Corey Dickerson, Vince DiMaggio, Mike Easler, Gene Freese, Dick Groat, J.A. Happ, Richie Hebner, Don Hoak, Brian Hunter, Mike LaValliere, Kenny Lofton, Andrew McCutchen, Jose Mesa, Charlie Morton, Brandon Moss, Terry Mulholland, Al Oliver, Dan Plesac, Bill Robinson, Matt Stairs, Dale Sveum, Frank Thomas, Bobby Tolan, Andy Van Slyke, Rick White, and Ty Wiggington have all played for both the Pittsburgh Pirates and the Philadelphia Phillies.

# CHAPTER 15:

# THE AWARDS SECTION

## QUIZ TIME!

1. Which Pittsburgh Pirates player won the National League MVP Award in 2013?

    a. Pedro Alvarez
    b. Andrew McCutchen
    c. Starling Marte
    d. Neil Walker

2. As of the end of the 2020 season, Jason Bay is the only Pittsburgh Pirates player to ever win the National League Rookie of the Year Award (2004).

    a. True
    b. False

3. How many Gold Glove Awards did Bill Mazeroski win during his time with the Pittsburgh Pirates?

    a. 4
    b. 6

c. 8

d. 10

4. Which player is the only Pittsburgh Pirates player to ever win the MLB All-Star Game MVP Award?

   a. Barry Bonds
   b. Willie Stargell
   c. Andrew McCutchen
   d. Dave Parker

5. Who are the only two Pittsburgh Pirates players to ever win the Roberto Clemente Award?

   a. A.J. Burnett and Andrew McCutchen
   b. Dave Parker and Andrew McCutchen
   c. Willie Stargell and Andrew McCutchen
   d. Dave Parker and Willie Stargell

6. Which Pittsburgh Pirates player won a Silver Slugger Award in 1988?

   a. Bobby Bonilla
   b. Andy Van Slyke
   c. Barry Bonds
   d. Both A & B

7. No Pittsburgh Pirates player has ever won the MLB Home Run Derby.

   a. True
   b. False

8. Which Pittsburgh Pirates player was named the DHL Hometown Hero? (Voted by MLB fans as the most outstanding player in franchise history.)

   a. Willie Stargell
   b. Roberto Clemente
   c. Ralph Kiner
   d. Dave Parker

9. Who was the first Pittsburgh Pirates player to win a National League Gold Glove Award?

   a. Bobby Shantz
   b. Roberto Clemente
   c. Harvey Haddix
   d. Bill Mazeroski

10. Who was the first Pittsburgh Pirates player to win a Silver Slugger Award?

    a. Don Robinson
    b. Bobby Bonilla
    c. Johnny Ray
    d. Rick Rhoden

11. Which Pittsburgh Pirates player won the 2013 Comeback Player of the Year Award?

    a. Russell Martin
    b. Clint Barmes
    c. Francisco Liriano
    d. A.J. Burnett

12. No Pittsburgh Pirates catcher OR first baseman has won a Silver Slugger Award.

   a. True
   b. False

13. Clint Hurdle was named the National League Manager in which year?

   a. 2012
   b. 2013
   c. 2014
   d. 2015

14. How many consecutive Silver Slugger Awards did Andrew McCutchen win during his time with the Pittsburgh Pirates?

   a. 2
   b. 3
   c. 4
   d. 5

15. Roberto Clemente won consecutive National League Gold Glove Awards with the Pittsburgh Pirates from 1961 to which year?

   a. 1969
   b. 1970
   c. 1971
   d. 1972

16. Jim Leyland was named the 1990 AND 1992 National League Manager of the Year.

a. True

b. False

17. Which Pittsburgh Pirates player was named the 1990 National League Cy Young Award winner?

a. Bob Walk

b. Neal Heaton

c. John Smiley

d. Doug Drabek

18. Which Pittsburgh Pirates player won a Silver Slugger Award in 1993?

a. Kevin Young

b. Jay Bell

c. Andy Van Slyke

d. All of the Above

19. Which Pittsburgh Pirates pitcher won the Trevor Hoffman NL Reliever of the Year Award in 2015?

a. Tony Watson

b. Antonio Bastardo

c. Mark Melancon

d. Jared Hughes

20. The Pittsburgh Pirates were named the 2015 Baseball America Organization of the Year.

a. True

b. False

# QUIZ ANSWERS

1. B – Andrew McCutchen

2. A – True

3. C – 8

4. D – Dave Parker

5. C – Willie Stargell and Andrew McCutchen

6. D – Both A & B

7. A – True

8. B – Roberto Clemente

9. D – Bill Mazeroski (1958)

10. A – Don Robinson (1982)

11. C – Francisco Liriano

12. A- True

13. B – 2013

14. C – 4 (2012-2015)

15. D – 1972

16. A – True

17. D – Doug Drabek

18. B – Jay Bell

19. C – Mark Melancon

20. A – True

# DID YOU KNOW?

1. The Pittsburgh Pirates have had 2 different players win Cy Young Awards in franchise history, Vern Law (1960) and Doug Drabek (1990).

2. The Pittsburgh Pirates have had 11 different players win Silver Slugger Awards in franchise history, Don Robinson, Rick Rhoden, Johnny Ray, Neil Walker, Pedro Alvarez, Jay Bell, Jack Wilson, Bobby Bonilla, Andy Van Slyke, Barry Bonds, and Andrew McCutchen.

3. The Pittsburgh Pirates have had only one player named National League Rookie of the Year in franchise history, Jason Bay (2004).

4. The Pittsburgh Pirates have had 17 different players win American League Gold Glove Awards in franchise history, Harvey Haddix, Bobby Shantz, Rick Reuschel, Tony Pena, Mike LaValliere, Bill Mazeroski, Jose Lind, Gene Alley, Jay Bell, Roberto Clemente, Bill Virdon, Dave Parker, Andy Van Slyke, Barry Bonds, Nate McLouth, Andrew McCutchen, and Corey Dickerson.

5. The Pittsburgh Pirates have had 7 different players win the National League MVP Award in franchise history, Paul Waner, Dick Groat, Roberto Clemente, Dave Parker, Willie Stargell, Barry Bonds, and Andrew McCutchen.

6. Russell Martin was named the 2014 Wilson Defensive Player of the Year. Starling Marte was named the 2015 Wilson Defensive Player of the Year.

7. The Pittsburgh Pirates have had only 1 player win the MLB All-Star Game MVP Award in franchise history, Dave Parker in 1979.

8. Bob Prince and Milo Hamilton are the two Pittsburgh Pirates Ford C. Frick Award recipients.

9. The Pittsburgh Pirates have had 2 different managers win the National League Manager of the Year Award in franchise history, Jim Leyland (1990 and 1992) and Clint Hurdle (2013).

10. The Pittsburgh Pirates have had 4 different players win the Comeback Player of the Year Award in franchise history, Vern Law (1964), Willie Stargell (1978), Rick Reuschel (1985), and Francisco Liriano (2013).

# CHAPTER 16:

# THE STEEL CITY

## QUIZ TIME!

1. Which Pittsburgh museum houses the world's first T-Rex skeleton?

   a. Fort Pitt Museum
   b. The Frick
   c. Carnegie Museum of Natural History
   d. Carnegie Science Center

2. The Polio Vaccine was created in Pittsburgh in 1950.

   a. True
   b. False

3. Which celebrity is NOT from Pittsburgh?

   a. Jeff Goldblum
   b. Mark Cuban
   c. Gene Kelly
   d. Beyonce

4. Which fast food staple was created in a suburb of Pittsburgh?

   a. Whopper
   b. Big Mac
   c. Frosty
   d. Double-Double

5. In 1920, what percentage of glass in the United States was made in Pittsburgh.

   a. 20
   b. 40
   c. 60
   d. 80

6. Pittsburgh has more of what, per capita than any other American city?

   a. Cars
   b. Dogs
   c. Bars
   d. All of the Above

7. Pittsburgh's "Bicycle Heaven" is the world's largest bike museum.

   a. True
   b. False

8. What is the name of Pittsburgh's NFL team?

   a. Pittsburgh 49ers
   b. Pittsburgh Steelers

c. Pittsburgh Raiders

d. Pittsburgh Jets

9. What is the name of Pittsburgh's NHL team?

a. Pittsburgh Sharks

b. Pittsburgh Penguins

c. Pittsburgh Wild

d. Pittsburgh Rangers

10. How many Super Bowl Championships do the Pittsburgh Steelers currently?

a. 2

b. 4

c. 6

d. 8

11. What is the name of the Pittsburgh Steelers' current stadium?

a. M&T Bank Stadium

b. Heinz Field

c. Arrowhead Stadium

d. State Farm Stadium

12. The Pittsburgh Penguins currently have 5 Stanley Cup Championships.

a. True

b. False

13. What is the name of the Pittsburgh Penguins' current arena?

a. T-Mobile Arena

b. SAP Center

c. United Center

d. PPG Paints Arena

14. For the 1943 season, the Pittsburgh Steelers and Philadelphia Eagles combined their teams due to not enough players. That season, they were known as the "Steagles".

a. True

b. False

15. Which NFL quarterback is not from Pittsburgh?

a. Joe Namath

b. Joe Montana

c. Dan Marino

d. Steve Young

16. The Soldiers and Sailors Memorial Hall in Pittsburgh is the largest memorial dedicated to all military branches in the United States.

a. True

b. False

17. How many bridges, the most in the world, does Pittsburgh have?

a. 436

b. 446

c. 456

d. 466

18. What is Pittsburgh International Airport's code?

    a. PIB
    b. PIA
    c. PIT
    d. PIG

19. Which movie was NOT filmed in Pittsburgh?

    a. The Avengers
    b. Dunkirk
    c. The Dark Night Rises
    d. Independence Day

20. The tallest education building in the Western Hemisphere is located at the University of Pittsburgh.

    a. True
    b. False

# QUIZ ANSWERS

1.  C – Carnegie Museum of Natural History

2.  A - True

3.  D – Beyonce

4.  B – Big Mac

5.  D – 80

6.  C – Bars

7.  A- True

8.  B – Pittsburgh Steelers

9.  B – Pittsburgh Penguins

10. C – 6

11. B – Heinz Field

12. A- True

13. D – PPG Paints Arena

14. A – True

15. D – Steve Young

16. A – True

17. B – 446

18. C – PIT

19. B – Dunkirk

20. A – True

# DID YOU KNOW?

1. The Andy Warhol Museum in Pittsburgh is the largest museum dedicated to a single artist in North America.

2. The Golden Gate Bridge, Empire State Building and several WWII ships were built using Pittsburgh steel.

3. In 1954, Pittsburgh's WQED was the first public TV station to go on air in the United States.

4. Pittsburgh has a lot of stairs. It currently has over 700 sets of public steps across the city.

5. Fred Rogers, better known as Mr. Rogers, was from Pittsburgh. His show was filmed and produced in Pittsburgh as well.

6. Pittsburgh ranks second all-time on the list of most sports championships by city… even without an NBA basketball team.

7. Pittsburgh is home to over 400 bridges.

8. Heinz Ketchup was invented in Pittsburgh.

9. Can pull-tabs were invented in Pittsburgh.

10. The first simultaneous heart, liver and kidney transplant took place at Presbyterian-University Hospital in Pittsburgh.

# CHAPTER 17:

# POPS

## QUIZ TIME!

1. What is Willie Stargell's full name?

   a. Donovan William Stargell

   b. William Donovan Stargell

   c. Dornel Wilver Stargell

   d. Wilver Dornel Stargell

2. Willie Stargell played his entire 21-season MLB career with the Pittsburgh Pirates.

   a. True

   b. False

3. Where was Willie Stargell born?

   a. Tulsa, Oklahoma

   b. Earlsboro, Oklahoma

   c. Lima, Ohio

   d. Cleveland, Ohio

4. When was Willie Stargell born?

a. May 6, 1940

b. May 6, 1945

c. March 6, 1940

d. March 6, 1945

5. Willie Stargell was named the 1979 National League MVP.

a. True

b. False

6. How many Gold Glove Awards did Willie Stargell win over the course of his 21-season MLB career?

a. 0

b. 1

c. 2

d. 3

7. What year was Willie Stargell inducted into the National Baseball Hall of Fame with 82.4% of the vote?

a. 1987

b. 1988

c. 1989

d. 1990

8. Willie Stargell was named the 1979 NLCS MVP.

a. True

b. False

9. How many World Series Championships did Willie Stargell win over the course of his 21-season MLB career?

a. 0

b. 1

c. 2

d. 3

10. What year did Willie Stargell make his MLB debut?

    a. 1955

    b. 1958

    c. 1960

    d. 1962

11. How many MLB All-Star Games was Willie Stargell named to over the course of his 21-season MLB career?

    a. 5

    b. 7

    c. 10

    d. 15

12. The Pittsburgh Pirates retired Willie Stargell's uniform No. 8 on September 6, 1982.

    a. True

    b. False

13. Willie Stargell won a Roberto Clemente Award in which year?

    a. 1972

    b. 1973

    c. 1974

    d. 1975

14. Willie Stargell was named the 1979 World Series MVP.

    a. True
    b. False

15. How many times was Willie Stargell named the National League Home Run leader?

    a. 1
    b. 2
    c. 3
    d. 4

16. What year was Willie Stargell named the National League RBI leader?

    a. 1968
    b. 1970
    c. 1973
    d. 1975

17. Willie Stargell was named the 1979 Major League Player of the Year.

    a. True
    b. False

18. How many home runs did Willie Stargell hit over the course of his 21-season MLB career?

    a. 455
    b. 475
    c. 485
    d. 495

19. How many RBIs did Willie Stargell collect over the course of his 21-season MLB career?

    a. 1,520
    b. 1,530
    c. 1,540
    d. 1,550

20. Willie Stargell's career batting average was .282.

    a. True
    b. False

# QUIZ ANSWERS

1. D – Wilver Dornel Stargell

2. A – True

3. B – Earlsboro, Oklahoma

4. C – March 6, 1940

5. A – True

6. A – 0

7. B – 1988

8. A – True

9. C – 2

10. D – 1962

11. B – 7

12. A – True

13. C – 1974

14. A – True

15. B – 2 (1971, 1973)

16. C – 1973

17. A – True

18. B – 475

19. C – 1,540

20. A – True

# DID YOU KNOW?

1.  Willie Stargell stole only 17 bases over the course of his 21-season MLB career.

2.  After his retirement from the MLB, Willie Stargell coached first base for the Atlanta Braves from 1986-1988.

3.  Two days before Willie Stargell's death, a statue of Stargell was unveiled at PNC Park.

4.  "When I played, there were 600 baseball players, and 599 of them loved Willie Stargell." – Joe Morgan

5.  Willie Stargell was named the NL Player of the Week once in his MLB career (May 8th, 1977). Willie Stargell was named the NL Player of the Month three times in his MLB career (June 1965, April 1971, June 1971).

6.  The Willie Stargell Foundation helps support research for kidney disease.

7.  Wilver "Willie" Stargell Avenue is located in Alameda, California where Stargell grew up and went to high school.

8.  Willie Stargell played alongside fellow MLB players Curt Motton and Tommy Harper while in high school.

9.  While playing for farm teams, Willie Stargell was not allowed to stay at the same hotels as his white teammates on the road. Black players were forced to stay in the poor black areas of the towns they were in.

10. Legendary Los Angeles Dodgers broadcaster Vin Scully referred to Willie Stargell by his given name, "Wilver" during broadcasts.

# CHAPTER 18:

# BARRY

## QUIZ TIME!

1. Where was Barry Bonds born?

    a. Las Vegas, Nevada

    b. Riverside, California

    c. Portland, Oregon

    d. Denver, Colorado

2. Barry Bonds is Reggie Jackson's cousin.

    a. True

    b. False

3. Barry Bonds played for the Pittsburgh Pirates for 7 seasons. He only played for one other MLB team in his career. Who was that one other team?

    a. Seattle Mariners

    b. New York Yankees

    c. San Francisco Giants

    d. Chicago White Sox

4. Barry Bonds holds the record for most intentional walks in MLB history. How many did he collect over the course of his career?

   a. 293
   b. 500
   c. 608
   d. 688

5. What year was Barry Bonds born?

   a. 1971
   b. 1965
   c. 1964
   d. 1969

6. How many times was Barry Bonds named the NL MVP over the course of his 22-season MLB career?

   a. 2
   b. 5
   c. 7
   d. 9

7. Barry Bonds is in the National Baseball Hall of Fame.

   a. True
   b. False

8. Where did Barry Bonds attend college?

   a. Arizona State University
   b. University of Arizona
   c. UC Riverside
   d. CSU Fullerton

9. How many times did Barry Bonds win the NL Batting Title over the course of his 22-season MLB career?

   a. 0
   b. 1
   c. 2
   d. 3

10. Barry Bonds served as a hitting coach for which team for one season?

    a. Miami Marlins
    b. San Francisco Giants
    c. Pittsburgh Pirates
    d. Los Angeles Angels

11. In 2002, Barry Bonds carried the torch at the Winter Olympics in which location?

    a. Nagano, Japan
    b. Vancouver, Canada
    c. Turin, Italy
    d. Salt Lake City, Utah

12. The San Francisco Giants retired Barry Bonds' number 25 on August 11, 2018, before a game against his former team, the Pittsburgh Pirates.

    a. True
    b. False

13. How many times was Barry Bonds named the Major League Player of the Year over the course of his 22-season MLB career?

a.  1

b.  2

c.  3

d.  4

14. Barry Bonds' father was a Major League Baseball player as well. What team did Bobby Bonds NOT play for during his 14-season MLB career?

    a.  San Francisco Giants

    b.  California Angels

    c.  Philadelphia Phillies

    d.  New York Yankees

15. What year did Barry Bonds play his final MLB game?

    a.  2005

    b.  2007

    c.  2010

    d.  2012

16. Barry Bonds hit a home run on every day between April 1-September 29 in his career, except for August 5. August 5 was the date his father, Bobby homered on the most.

    a.  True

    b.  False

17. Barry Bonds holds the all-time MLB Home Run record. He passed Hank Aaron on the list in 2007. How many total home runs did Barry Bonds hit during his career?

    a.  755

    b.  759

c. 762

d. 803

18. How many MLB All-Star Games was Barry Bonds named to over the course of his 22-season MLB career?

    a. 8

    b. 12

    c. 14

    d. 16

19. How many Gold Glove Awards did Barry Bond win over the course of his 22-season MLB career?

    a. 2

    b. 5

    c. 6

    d. 8

20. Barry Bonds won 12 Silver Slugger Awards over the course of his 22-season MLB career.

    a. True

    b. False

# QUIZ ANSWERS

1. B – Riverside, California

2. A – True

3. C – San Francisco Giants

4. D – 688

5. C – 1964

6. C – 7

7. B – False

8. A – Arizona State University

9. C – 2

10. A – Miami Marlins

11. D – Salt Lake City, Utah

12. A – True

13. C – 3

14. C – Philadelphia Phillies

15. B – 2007

16. A – True

17. C – 762

18. C – 14

19. D – 8

20. A – True

# DID YOU KNOW?

1.  Barry Bonds is a 3x NL Hank Aaron Award winner (2001, 2002, 2004).

2.  Barry Bonds is a 2x NL Home Run leader (1993, 2001) and NL RBI leader (1993).

3.  Barry Bonds won an ESPN ESPY Award for "Male Athlete of the Year" in 1994.

4.  After Bonds' playing career ended, he was investigated for the use of steroids. He was put on trial and sentenced to two years of probation, 30 days house arrest, 250 hours of community service, and was charged a $4,000 fine.

5.  Barry Bonds has made a few TV and movie appearances. He starred in the movie *Rookie of the Year* as himself. He also made TV appearances on *Beverly Hills 90210* and *Nash Bridges*.

6.  Barry Bonds also played basketball and football while in high school.

7.  Barry Bonds was drafted by the Giants out of high school but decided to pass and attended Arizona State instead. He was then drafted by the Pirates out of college and made his way back to San Francisco in the end.

8.  Barry Bonds graduated from Arizona State University in 1986 with a degree in Criminology. He was named the

ASU On Deck Circle Most Valuable Player. He was not well-liked by his Sun Devil teammates due to being self-centered.

9. Bonds was known for being difficult, ungrateful, and filled with attitude. He has mentioned that he now regrets his behavior and the way he treated press. He claims he could have had more endorsements if he had behaved in a kinder manner.

10. Bonds was the oldest player (38) to win the National League Batting Title in 2002.

# CHAPTER 19:

# AMERICA'S PASTIME

## QUIZ TIME!

1. How many total teams play in Major League Baseball?

   a. 15
   b. 20
   c. 30
   d. 33

2. Major League Baseball was founded in 1903.

   a. True
   b. False

3. Who is the current commissioner of Major League Baseball?

   a. Bart Giamatti
   b. Fay Vincent
   c. Bud Selig
   d. Rob Manfred

4. What year was the National League founded?

a. 1870

b. 1876

c. 1903

d. 1911

5. What year was the American League founded?

a. 1888

b. 1901

c. 1903

d. 1918

6. Major League Baseball is the second wealthiest professional sports league. Which league is the wealthiest?

a. NBA

b. NHL

c. NFL

d. MLS

7. The Major League Baseball headquarters is located in New York City.

a. True

b. False

8. How many games does each Major League Baseball team play per season?

a. 92

b. 122

c. 162

d. 192

9. In which two U.S. states is Major League Baseball's Spring Training held?

    a. California and Florida

    b. Arizona and Florida

    c. Arizona and California

    d. California and Arizona

10. How many stitches does a Major League Baseball baseball have?

    a. 98

    b. 100

    c. 108

    d. 110

11. Where is the National Baseball Hall of Fame located?

    a. Denver, Colorado

    b. Phoenix, Arizona

    c. Los Angeles, California

    d. Cooperstown, New York

12. All 30 Major League Baseball teams are located in the United States.

    a. True

    b. False

13. Which current Major League Baseball stadium is the oldest baseball stadium still in use?

    a. Angel Stadium

    b. Dodger Stadium

c. Fenway Park

d. Wrigley Field

14. Major League Baseball has the highest attendance of any sports league in the world.

a. True

b. False

15. Fill in the blank: Seventh Inning _____

a. Jog

b. Song

c. Shake

d. Stretch

16. William Howard Taft was the first United States president to throw out the ceremonial first pitch at a Major League Baseball game.

a. True

b. False

17. It is a Major League Baseball rule that all umpires must wear what color underwear in case they rip their pants?

a. Tan

b. Gray

c. White

d. Black

18. What year did the first Major League Baseball World Series take place?

a. 1903

b. 1905

c. 1915

d. 1920

19. Former Major League Baseball Commissioner, Bart Giamatti is the father of actor, Paul Giamatti.

    a. True

    b. False

20. The song traditionally played in the middle of the 7th inning at Major League Baseball games is called *Take Me Out to the Ballpark.*

    a. True

    b. False

# QUIZ ANSWERS

1. C – 30

2. A - True

3. D – Rob Manfred

4. B – 1876

5. B – 1901

6. C – NFL

7. A- True

8. C – 162

9. B – Arizona and Florida

10. C – 108

11. D – Cooperstown, New York

12. B – False, 29 out of 30 (The Toronto Blue Jays are located in Canada)

13. C – Fenway Park

14. A – True

15. D – Stretch

16. A – True

17. D – Black

18. A - 1903

19. A – True

20. B – False, *Take Me Out to the Ballgame*

# DID YOU KNOW?

1. The average lifespan of a baseball in a Major League Baseball game is 5-7 pitches. This means approximately 5-6 dozen baseballs are used in every Major League Baseball game.

2. The Boston Americans won the very first Major League Baseball World Series. They defeated the Pittsburgh Pirates in 8 games. Today the most games a World Series can go is 7.

3. The New York Yankees currently hold the most World Series titles in Major League Baseball with 27 total.

4. Hot dogs are the most popular food item sold at Major League Baseball ballparks. Over 21 million hot dogs were sold at MLB stadiums in 2014.

5. The longest Major League Baseball game on record occurred on May 9, 1984 between the Chicago White Sox and Milwaukee Brewers. The game lasted 8 hours, 6 minutes. The most innings played in a Major League Baseball game were 26 innings on May 1, 1920. The game was between the Brooklyn Dodgers and Boston Braves.

6. The mound to home plate distance at Major League Baseball ballparks is 60 feet, 6 inches.

7. Before they can be used in a Major League Baseball game, each MLB baseball is rubbed with a special mud to

improve grip and reduce luster. This special mud comes from a specific, secret location in the state of New Jersey.

8. The fastest Major League Baseball game on record took place on September 28, 1919. The game between the New York Giants and Philadelphia Phillies took 51 minutes. An average MLB game is 3 hours.

9. The American League uses a designated hitter. A DH only hits and does not play in the field. In the National League, the pitcher hits instead of using a designated hitter. If an interleague game is being played, whether a DH is used or not is determined by which team is the home team. If the home team is from the American League, each team will use a DH. If the home team is from the National League, each team's pitcher will hit.

10. The distance between each of the four bases in Major League Baseball is 90 feet.

# CONCLUSION

Learn anything new? Now you truly are the ultimate Pirates fan! Not only did you learn about the Bucs of the modern era, but you also expanded your knowledge back to the early days of the franchise.

You learned about the Pittsburgh Pirates' history, from their origins right through to modern day, beginning of the year 2021. You learned about the history of their uniforms and jersey numbers and read some of the craziest nicknames of all time. You learned more about the legendary Barry Bonds and Dave Parker. You also learned about the Hall of Famers Roberto Clemente and Willie Stargell.

You were amazed by Bucs stats and recalled some of the most infamous Pirates trades, drafts, and draft picks of all time. You broke down your knowledge by outfielders, infielders, pitchers, and catchers. You looked back on the Pirates' championships, playoff feats and the awards that came before, after, and during them. You also learned about the Pirates' fiercest rivalries both within their division and out.

Every team in the MLB has a storied history, but the Pittsburgh Pirates have one of the most memorable of all.

They have won 5 World Series Championships with the backing of their devoted fans. Being the ultimate Pirates fan takes knowledge and a whole lot of patience, which you tested with this book. Whether you knew every answer or were stumped by several questions, you learned some of the most baffling history that the game of baseball has to offer.

The deep history of the Pittsburgh Pirates franchise represents what we all love about the game of baseball. The heart, the determination, the tough times, and the unexpected moments, plus the players that inspire us and encourage us to do our best because even if you get knocked down, there is always another game and another day.

With players like Colin Moran, Bryan Reynolds, and Adam Frazier, the future for the Pittsburgh Pirates continues to look bright. They have a lot to prove but there is no doubt that this franchise will continue to be one of the most competitive teams in Major League Baseball year after year.

It's a new decade which means there is a clean slate, ready to continue writing the history of the Pittsburgh Pirates. The ultimate Pirates fan cannot wait to see what's to come for their beloved Bucs.

www.ingramcontent.com/pod-product-compliance
Lightning Source LLC
Chambersburg PA
CBHW060232030426
42335CB00014B/1426